THE MOST SIGNIFICANT
TEACHINGS
IN THE
BIBLE

Also by Christopher D. Hudson

The Quickview Bible

*The Most Significant People, Places,
and Events in the Bible*

THE MOST SIGNIFICANT TEACHINGS IN THE BIBLE

CHRISTOPHER D. HUDSON
WITH LEN WOODS

ZONDERVAN ACADEMIC

ZONDERVAN ACADEMIC

The Most Significant Teachings in the Bible
Copyright © 2019 by Christopher D. Hudson

Requests for information should be addressed to:
Zondervan, *3900 Sparks Dr. SE, Grand Rapids, Michigan 49546*

Library of Congress Cataloging-in-Publication Data

Names: Hudson, Christopher D, author.
Title: The most significant teachings in the Bible / Christopher Hudson.
Description: Grand Rapids : Zondervan, 2019.
Identifiers: LCCN 2019009077 (print) | LCCN 2019980419 (ebook) | ISBN 9780310566182 (paperback) | ISBN
    9780310566199 (ebook)
Subjects: LCSH: Bible--Miscellanea. | Bible--Introductions.
Classification: LCC BS538 .H67 2019 (print) | LCC BS538 (ebook) | DDC 220.6--dc23
LC record available at https://lccn.loc.gov/2019009077 LC ebook record available at https://lccn.loc.gov/2019980419

Produced with the assistance of Hudson Bible (www. HudsonBible.com).

Cover design: Tammy Johnson
Cover and interior illustration: Christopher Hudson, www.HudsonBible.com

Printed in the United States

21 22 23 24 25 26 27 28 29 30 31 32 33 /LSC/ 20 19 18 17 16 15 14 13 12 11 10 9 8 7 6

To the Hudson Bible team

*It is an honor to work together as we
create resources that help people read,
engage, and apply the Bible*

"Lord, to whom shall we go?
You have the words of eternal life."

John 6:68

CONTENTS

Part 9: Living as a Christian

INTRODUCTION

People call the Bible many things: the Word of God, Scripture, Holy Writ, the Good Book. Augustine even called this ancient collection of sacred documents our "letters from home."

Here's a valid question: Why should we read this hodgepodge of Jewish history and law, Christian sermons, and personal letters? The Bible was written by about forty different authors over a period of perhaps fifteen hundred years. What's the relevance of an old book that often feels more like a national scrapbook with its tabernacle plans and genealogies, its hymns and prayers, its prophecies and census records?

Here's why the Bible deserves your attention:

It claims to be divinely inspired. Many books are *inspiring*. The Bible says it is *inspired*— the authoritative, trustworthy words of God (2 Timothy 3:16), delivered to and through Spirit-guided human authors.

It shows all that God has done to rescue mankind and restore the world. The Old Testament prophesies the coming of a Messiah (i.e., Savior/King). The New Testament powerfully shows Jesus to be that promised Divine One (John 20:31; 1 John 5:13).

It is the greatest power on earth. God's good news is able to save those who are far from God (Romans 1:16). Not only this, but his Word can make people pure and give them power over sin (Psalm 119:9, 11; John 17:17). In the prophecy of Jeremiah, we read these words: "'Is not my word like fire,' declares the LORD, 'and like a hammer that breaks a rock in pieces?'"(23:29). Countless believers throughout history would testify that God's Word both shattered their hard hearts and healed their broken hearts.

It contains valuable warnings about how—and how not—to live. It teaches us valuable lessons from the lives (good and bad) of those who have gone before us (1 Corinthians 10:11).

It equips us for a life of wisdom and purpose. The Bible not only reminds us of what is true but also shows us where we are wrong and instructs us how to get back on track (2 Timothy 3:16).

While the Bible speaks on many topics, this book will help you digest some of the most important teaching on the following topics:

- Getting to know God
- Living in our world
- Marriage and family

- Friends, neighbors, and enemies
- Work, money, and business
- Struggles and suffering
- The supernatural
- Sin and the solution
- Living as a Christian

In all these ways and more, the wisdom of the Bible continues to change lives. No wonder Paul wrote, "For everything that was written in the past was written to teach us, so that through the endurance taught in the Scriptures and the encouragement they provide we might have hope" (Romans 15:4).

My hope is that you will read the Bible for what it says, engage what God is saying, and apply it deeply in your life.

Christopher D. Hudson
www.ReadEngageApply.com
Twitter: @ReadEngageApply
Facebook.com/Christopher.D.Hudson.books

PART 1

GETTING TO KNOW GOD

CHAPTER 1

When people speak of God, they often mention his *love*, his *power*, or his *grace*. Rarely do they speak of his *holiness*.

The *consequences* of God's holiness. The words *holy* and *holiness* are found more than six hundred times in the Bible. Clearly this is not a minor topic.

The word *holy* conveys the idea of "separateness." Holy things are sacred, not profane; they are pure as opposed to impure. When the Bible speaks of the holiness of God, it means that his nature is flawless and his actions are always perfect. He is set apart from sin and all things unclean.

Because God is the very essence of purity, sin is always an affront to him. What's more, it ruins the creatures he loves and contaminates the world he has made. As a good surgeon refuses to work in a germ-infested operating room, so God has zero tolerance for sin.

The *cure* for unholiness. By sending Jesus to take the sin of the world upon himself (2 Corinthians 5:21) and experience the judgment (i.e., separation from God) all sinners deserve (Romans 5:8), God is able to make believers holy (Ephesians 5:25–26; Hebrews 13:12).

The *calling* to be holy. Here is a stunning theological reality: God regards those with faith in Jesus—here and now—as holy. Believers actually get credit for Jesus's perfect life. This is why the New Testament repeatedly calls Christians God's "holy people" (Romans 1:7; 1 Corinthians 1:2). However, we aren't just *called* holy; we're called *to be* holy. Holiness is supposed to be a lifestyle. Paul put it this way: "For God did not call us to be impure, but to live a holy life" (1 Thessalonians 4:7). Peter said it like this: "Just as he who called you is holy, so be holy in all you do" (1 Peter 1:15). How is this even possible? By the power of the *Holy* Spirit (Galatians 5:22–23).

Life Application

If someone gave us a glass of toxic waste, we would never drink it. But what if they added an eyedropper full of the purest water on earth? Would we drink it then? What if the glass was full of pure water and someone added just a drop or two of toxic waste— would we drink it then? There's no such thing as "sort of" holy.

THE HOLINESS OF GOD

God's Holiness

God's holiness is a theme throughout Scripture. Here are themes from the book of Numbers which reveal God's high standards for his people.

God tells the Kohathites not to look at the holy things or they will die *4:17–20*

God commands the Israelites to put outside the camp anyone with a skin disease or discharge, or who is ceremonially unclean *5:1–4*

God's presence covers the tabernacle as a cloud *9:15–23*

God strikes the Israelites with a plague after they complain about the manna and grumble for meat *11:4–34*

God strikes Miriam with leprosy after she and Aaron speak against Moses *12*

God commands that a man who broke the Sabbath be stoned to death *15:32–36*

God instructs the Israelites to attach tassels to their garments as a reminder of his holiness *15:37–41*

God destroys Korah and his followers for speaking against Moses and Aaron *16:1–35*

God orders the deaths of the Israelites who worship the Baal of Peor *25*

God instructs the Israelites to drive out the Canaanites and destroy their idols and high places *33:50–56*

CROSS-REFERENCES

Exodus 19:6

Leviticus 20:26

Hebrews 12:14

CHAPTER 2

Some people want to read, engage, and apply the Bible but are intimidated by its 770,000 plus words divided into 31,000 verses and nearly 1,200 chapters. What are we supposed to do with this ancient library of sixty-six divinely inspired books?

By reading God's Word, we get to know God better. Each page reveals his character and tells us a little more about his plan. By engaging God while reading, we find that his Word changes, transforms, and revitalizes us.

Here are ten ways to engage the Bible:

1. **Listen to it.** Listen to others read, teach, and preach God's Word (Nehemiah 8:3; Luke 24:27).

2. **Read it ourselves.** By reading just three chapters a day, and four on Sundays, we can read the entire Bible in one year. For most of us, this is a commitment of only fifteen minutes a day.

3. **Learn to study it.** A number of tools are available to help us study the Bible, such as study Bibles, commentaries, and Bible dictionaries. Psalm 119 mentions the three steps of basic Bible study. Verse 18 talks about *observation*. This is where we probe a text like a detective, asking, "What do I see?" Verse 27 talks about *interpretation*. This is where we ponder a text prayerfully and carefully, asking, "What does it mean?" Verse 11 speaks directly to *application*: "What should I do?" By placing God's Word in our hearts, we look for ways to honor God by how we live.

4. **Memorize it** (Psalms 37:31; 119:11). By storing God's words in our hearts and minds, we are able to summon them in hard or tempting situations and find comfort and strength. Jesus did this when he was tempted by Satan in the desert.

5. **Meditate on it** (Joshua 1:8). Meditation is the process of patiently reflecting on a biblical truth to deepen our understanding of it.

6. **Discuss it.** Gather with some friends or join a small group to bat around the implications of Scripture for our lives (Ephesians 5:19).

Life Application

What do we mean when we say that the Bible is inspired? Inspiration is the process whereby the Spirit of God supernaturally guided the human authors of Scripture so that in the words of their original writings they composed and recorded without error God's message to mankind.

THE BIBLE AS GOD'S WORD

7. **Teach it to others** (Colossians 3:16). The old saying is true: the way to understand a subject better is to teach it to others. As we share with others, God's Spirit works through us to reveal his Word to them as well.

8. **Pray the Bible.** Praying Scripture is a spiritual discipline in which we turn the words of a Bible passage into a prayer—perhaps praise, perhaps petition. But even if we don't do that, there are hundreds of prayers in the Bible— for example, Ephesians 1:15–23 and 3:14–21—that we can make our own.

9. **Sing the Bible** (Colossians 3:16). The Psalms were originally sung, and many praise choruses and Scripture songs can help us learn truths about God and remind others of the gospel.

10. **Do the Bible.** James 1:22 talks about doing the Word. This means putting God's truth into practice—living it out. It's important to remember that God didn't give us his Word simply to make us more knowledgeable (or, God forbid, prideful), but to make us more like Jesus.

Characteristics of God's Word found in Psalms and the number of verses in which each trait appears

CROSS-REFERENCES

Matthew 4:4

John 17:17

Romans 15:4

CHAPTER 3

Hang around an older Christian and you'll eventually hear words and phrases like "God-fearing" or "the fear of the Lord." What does such talk mean? Why on earth should anyone be afraid of a loving God who sent his Son on a rescue mission to seek and save lost people (Luke 19:10; John 3:16)?

What is "the fear of the Lord"? That Hebrew word translated "fear" in verses like Deuteronomy 10:20 ("Fear the LORD your God and serve him") can have different nuances. It sometimes means "to be terrified or filled with dread" (due to the threat of judgment). It also conveys the idea of being overwhelmed with a sense of awe and reverence (Psalm 33:8).

What does a "God-fearing" person feel? When the characters of Scripture experience the majesty of God, reverent fear or respectful awe is *always* the response. People draw back and fall to the ground (John 18:6). They tremble (Exodus 19:16; 20:18) and beg for relief. This is because the glory of God is weighty (that's the literal meaning of the Hebrew word for *glory*). God's holiness has a shattering effect on sinners. Isaiah felt this kind of heavy dread. He spoke of being ruined or coming undone (Isaiah 6:5).

Why do we cultivate fear of the Lord? Having a proper sense of awe at the person and presence of God is good and healthy. We develop this kind of holy respect through hearing God's words (Deuteronomy 4:10; 17:19). The Bible demonstrates that fear of the Lord fosters faith and commitment to his purposes (Exodus 14:31). This deep reverence also sparks obedience (Deuteronomy 6:2) and typically culminates in gratitude and praise (Psalm 22:23). It leads to wise living (Proverbs 9:10) and the blessing of God (Psalms 115:13; 128:1; Proverbs 22:4).

Life Application

What are some signs that a person could use some "holy fear of God"? A cavalier attitude about sin. An irreverent view of the gospel. A cynical or mocking perspective on spiritual matters. Disdain for things that God values. Disregard of (or disobedience to) the clear teaching of God's Word.

A central theme in the book of Psalms is the fear of the Lord. The image on the next page reveals God's promises for those who fear him.

Fear of the Lord

The book of Psalms recounts spiritual blessings for those who fear and honor the Lord; here are the recurring reminders of what they will receive:

9

Receive God's salvation and protection

9

Receive God's blessings and provision

8

Receive God's commands

6

Receive God's love and compassion

CROSS-REFERENCES

Proverbs 14:27

Isaiah 50:10

2 Corinthians 5:11

CHAPTER 4

In his bestseller *What's So Amazing about Grace?* author Philip Yancey tells a story about a group of religious scholars who were debating the primary difference between Christianity and the other great religions of the world. When C. S. Lewis wandered into the room and realized what the discussion was about, he reportedly said, "Oh, that's easy. It's grace."

Grace has been explained in a myriad of ways: "Divine benevolence to the unworthy." "Unmerited favor." "Undeserved blessing." "God's kindness."

All of these distinctions and descriptions are true. The Bible says humans are natural-born sinners—enemies of God (Romans 3:23). Because of our refusal to honor and glorify God, we justly deserve death (Romans 6:23). However, in a shocking twist, God sent his Son, Jesus, to die in our place. Instead of death, we are offered life (Romans 5:8–11). *This* is the miracle and mystery of grace.

What else does the New Testament reveal about God's amazing grace?

- Jesus is the personification of grace (John 1:14).
- The gospel of Jesus is therefore grounded in grace (Acts 20:24).
- Grace is always a gift, never a reward (Romans 4:4).

- Sinners are saved by grace (Ephesians 2:8–9).
- God's grace is more than enough for all our sins and troubles (Romans 5:20; Hebrews 4:16).
- Recipients of God's grace are to show grace to others (1 Peter 4:10).
- Our conversations should be full of grace (Colossians 4:6).
- Humility is what opens the door for God's grace (James 4:6).

Life Application

Many get uncomfortable at the shocking doctrine of God's grace. The Almighty choosing to save sinners with no strings attached? Promising eternal life to all who believe (without first extracting promises from those people)? Isn't that dangerous? Doesn't the teaching of grace (i.e., God *giving* salvation rather than humans *earning* and *maintaining* their salvation) lead to an "anything goes" lifestyle? Not at all. According to Paul, grace "teaches us to say 'No' to ungodliness" (Titus 2:12).

GOD'S AMAZING GRACE

The Grace of God

Need examples of God's Grace? Look at a series of snapshots from the book of Isaiah.

He comforts his exiled people and tells them their sins have been paid for 40:1–2

He gives strength to the weary and power to the weak 40:29

He will protect the Israelites from their enemies 41:11–16

He chose Israel from the farthest ends of the earth to serve him 41:8–10

He will redeem Israel as his own 43:1

He provides water in the wilderness and streams in the wasteland 43:20

He will restore the towns of Judah 44:26

He has carried the Israelites since birth and will sustain them until they are old 46:3–4

He will go before the Israelites and guard them from behind 52:12

He will restore the land and free the captives 49:8–9

He has sent his Son to die for the sins of people 53:5

He will no longer be angry with his people 54:7–9

He will give an everlasting name to those who obey him 56:4–5

He will have mercy on his people and pardon them 55:7

He will create new heavens and a new earth 65:17

He will give his people a new name 62:1–4

His Spirit will not depart from Israel 59:21

He delays his wrath 48:9

CROSS-REFERENCES

Romans 3:24

Ephesians 4:7

2 Thessalonians 2:16

CHAPTER 5

GETTING TO KNOW GOD

Say the word *worship* and many immediately think of singing "worship songs" in special rooms designated for "worship services" at certain times of the week. But is that an accurate description of what the Bible means by worship?

The meaning of *worship*. One of the most common Old Testament words for *worship* means "to bow down." This Hebrew verb conveys the idea of showing honor, expressing devotion, or paying homage.

Our English word *worship* is actually a shortened form of the word *worthship*, which means "the state of having worth or value." Strictly speaking, *worship* is not a "religious" term. When we devote our time, energy, money, and emotion to something (or someone), we are saying, "Here is what I value." You could say we are *worshiping* that thing (or person), even if we never literally bow down to it.

The universality of worship. Since worship is a question of what (or whom) a person values, nobody can truthfully say, "I'm not into worship." Nineteenth-century English theologian Frederick Robertson put it this way: "It is not a thing which a man can decide, whether he will be a worshiper or not, a worshiper he *must* be, the only question is *what* will he worship? Every man worships—is a born worshiper."

The object of worship. The Bible calls people to see the one true God as the great worth or value of the universe and to live for his glory (Isaiah 40:25). We are to love our Creator—not lesser, created things—with all of our hearts (Deuteronomy 6:5; Romans 1:20–23). This means giving God our primary attention, allegiance, and affection.

To sum up, worship is a mindset and a lifestyle. It's the moment-by-moment practice of lifting our eyes to heaven and saying from the heart, "Lord, I want to live right here and right now in a way that brings you honor."

Life Application

Someone has said that we can tell what we worship (i.e., value most in life) by

- looking at our calendars,
- considering where our minds naturally wander when we're not otherwise engaged,
- listening to what comes out of our mouths,
- examining how we spend money, and
- noting what thrills us (when it happens) or angers us (when it doesn't).

WORSHIPING GOD

Worship Exercise

The top ten words of worship used by the writers of Psalms and the number of times they appear

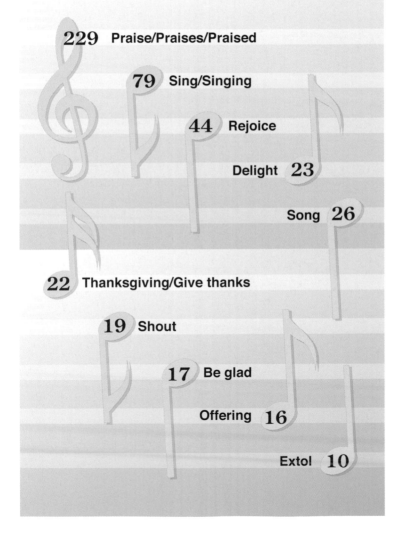

229 Praise/Praises/Praised

79 Sing/Singing

44 Rejoice

Delight **23**

Song **26**

22 Thanksgiving/Give thanks

19 Shout

17 Be glad

Offering **16**

Extol **10**

CROSS-REFERENCES

Exodus 34:14

Isaiah 44:6–23

1 Corinthians 10:31

CHAPTER 6

God is love (1 John 4:7). So how do we reconcile that truth with various biblical statements that declare that God "hates" certain things?

The meaning of *hate*. The Hebrew word most commonly translated "hate" in the Old Testament conveys the idea of detesting or loathing something so much that one is unwilling to put up with it and is hostile toward it. The word is used of the feeling people instinctively have for a sworn enemy.

How can a loving God *hate*? God hates the sinful actions of those who make it their mission to oppose his righteous rule, his perfect plan, or his precious people. In addition to the famous list of seven things that God hates in Proverbs 6:16–19, the Bible mentions—in other passages—certain hurtful attitudes and actions that arouse God's ire.

While these seven things create a good list, consider these other traits that God also hates: idolatry (Deuteronomy 12:31; 16:22; Jeremiah 44:4); unrepentant, evil people (Psalm 5:5; Hosea 9:15); violent people (Psalm 11:5); empty religious ritual (Isaiah 1:14; Amos 5:21); robbery and wrongdoing (Isaiah 61:8); those who challenge his authority (Jeremiah 12:8); and evil plans and perjury (Zechariah 8:17).

God hates evil because he is a good judge who wants to eradicate suffering, injustice, and evil. Although Jesus did say that Christians are to be known by their lavish love for one another (John 13:34–35) and by the way we love our enemies (Matthew 5:43–44), the Bible is also clear that believers are to hate evil (Amos 5:15; Romans 12:9; Hebrews 1:9).

Life Application

In Deuteronomy 1:27, Moses talked about how the Israelites grumbled when God led them on the difficult journey from Egypt to the promised land of Canaan. They even ascribed their trials to this ludicrous notion: "The LORD hates us; so he brought us out of Egypt . . . to destroy us."

Such thinking—then or now—is a blasphemous lie. God might hate sin, but he loves his people with a "love that surpasses knowledge" (Ephesians 3:19).

SEVEN THINGS GOD HATES

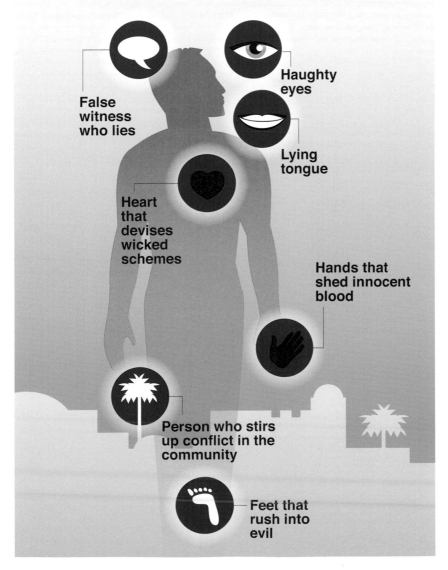

7 Things God Hates
Proverbs 6:16–19

False witness who lies

Haughty eyes

Lying tongue

Heart that devises wicked schemes

Hands that shed innocent blood

Person who stirs up conflict in the community

Feet that rush into evil

CROSS-REFERENCES

Amos 5:15

Malachi 2:16

Romans 9:13

Revelation 2:6

CHAPTER 7

More and more Christians (and churches) are engaging in ministries to the poor. They see such actions as consistent with a parable Jesus told about the priority of feeding and clothing the less fortunate, of taking in strangers, and of visiting prisoners (Matthew 25:34–46). Others question the wisdom of some charity efforts, fearing that in our desire to help, we sometimes inadvertently make the poor more dependent and perpetuate cycles of poverty. What does the Bible say?

Poverty isn't going anywhere. "You will always have the poor among you" (John 12:8), Jesus famously said. This doesn't mean we shouldn't try to help, but it does mean that in a broken world, the effects of sin and the systemic structures of poverty run deep. When God told the Israelites, "There need be no poor people among you" (Deuteronomy 15:4), he was speaking about what *could* be, not necessarily what *will* be—at least not until Jesus returns.

God has a heart for the poor and powerless. The Bible says that God raises the poor from the dust and the needy from the ash heap (1 Samuel 2:8; cf. Psalm 113:7). As the hands and feet (and mouths) of Jesus in the world, Christians are called to speak up for those who are destitute and cannot speak for themselves (Proverbs 31:8–9).

God wants to use his people to address poverty. God's Old Testament people were given multiple, highly detailed instructions for helping their countrymen who became poor (Leviticus 25:35). The better-off were to see to it that the poor received justice (Exodus 23:3, 6; Leviticus 19:15). At harvesttime, they were to leave some of their crop for the poor to glean (Leviticus 19:10). "Do not be hardhearted or tightfisted toward them. Rather be openhanded and freely lend them whatever they need. . . . Give generously to them . . . without a grudging heart" (Deuteronomy 15:7–8, 10). This sort of generous kindness "honors God" (Proverbs 14:31) and results in divine reward (Proverbs 19:17).

Life Application

Consider these warnings to those who neglect or mistreat the poor:

- "One who oppresses the poor to increase his wealth and one who gives gifts to the rich—both come to poverty" (Proverbs 22:16).
- "Those who give to the poor will lack nothing, but those who close their eyes to them receive many curses" (Proverbs 28:27).

GOD'S COMPASSION FOR THE NEEDY

God's Care for the Poor and Needy

The book of Psalms speaks to God's actions on behalf of those in need. Here are the number of verses from Psalms that tell of the ways God cares for those in need.

|||| |||| |||| |||| 19
Rescues/Protects

|||| | 6
Defends

|||| | 6
Provides/Blesses

||| 3
Remembers/Hears

|| 2
Sustains/Heals

CROSS-REFERENCES

Deuteronomy 15:11

Acts 9:36

James 2:2–6

CHAPTER 8

GETTING TO KNOW GOD

According to the apostle John, Jesus did so many spectacular things that if the whole world were one big library, it still wouldn't be big enough to contain all the books that could be written about Jesus (John 21:25).

The only proper response to such a life is, "Who *is* this?" Jesus actually asked his followers this very question: "Who do you say I am?" (Luke 9:20).

The one who called himself "the good shepherd" (John 10:14) and "the way and the truth and the life" (John 14:6) asked other questions too. Each one hints at who he really was, and each demands an answer:

- "What do you want me to do for you?" (Matthew 20:32).
- "Why are you troubled, and why do doubts rise in your minds?" (Luke 24:38).
- "What good is it for someone to gain the whole world, yet forfeit their soul?" (Mark 8:36).
- "Why do you call me, 'Lord, Lord,' and do not do what I say?" (Luke 6:46).
- "Do you love me?" (John 21:16).
- "Who is greater, the one seated at the table or the one who serves?" (Luke 22:27)

- "You of little faith, why are you so afraid?" (Matthew 8:26)
- "Is not life more than food, and the body more than clothes?" (Matthew 6:25)
- "Do you believe that I am able to do this?" (Matthew 9:28)
- "Why do you entertain evil thoughts in your hearts?" (Matthew 9:4)
- "But what about you? . . . Who do you say I am?" (Matthew 16:15)

If Jesus is divine, then these questions become some of the most important and urgent questions we can ever answer. Spend some time reviewing the accompanying image and references and further develop your own answers.

Life Application

What one big question still bugs you about Jesus? When have you felt closest to Christ in your life? Who do you believe Jesus is? What does your answer to that question mean for your life?

CROSS-REFERENCES

Luke 8:25

John 5:6; 11:25–26

WHO IS JESUS CHRIST?

Who Is Jesus Christ?

Many people think that Jesus Christ was simply a great teacher. But Christians believe that he was far more than a mere human being. His death and resurrection radically changed the course of history. Christ's love allows people to enter into a true and meaningful relationship with God the Father.

Jesus is . . .

FULLY HUMAN
- He was born as a human baby
- He endured the pains and temptations of humanity
- He suffered a physical and humiliating death

Mk 1:12–13; Lk 2:1–21; Php 2:5–8

SINLESS
- He did not sin, even when tempted
- He was undeserving of punishment and death

Mt 4:1–11; Heb 4:15

FULLY DIVINE
- He is the Son of God
- He is God incarnate, the "Word" made flesh, who came to earth to redeem humanity

Jn 1:1,14; 20:31

THE MESSIAH
- He is the Messiah foretold in Old Testament prophecies
- His kingdom is the kingdom of God, where his followers from all nations are united in love and peace

Isa 53; Mic 5:2; Mk 14:61–62; Jn 4:25–42; 18:36

THE SAVIOR
- Though sinless, he chose to die and receive humanity's punishment for their sin, in order to save them
- Through his resurrection, he conquered death and sin, Satan and hell
- He promises eternal life to those who believe in him

Lk 24:5–7; Jn 3:16,36; 5:24; ll:25; Heb 9:14

THE LAST ADAM
- He provides forgiveness and new life, abolishing the sin and death that Adam brought upon humanity

Ge 3; Ro 5:12–21; 1Co 15:21–22,45–49

THE HIGH PRIEST
- He directly connects people to God
- He was the perfect, sinless, ultimate sacrifice for sin; no other sacrifice or priest is needed for forgiveness from God

Heb 3:1; 4:14–15; 7:24–27

CHAPTER 9

GETTING TO KNOW GOD

One of the foundational beliefs of Christianity is that Jesus was (and is) God incarnate, that is, God in a human body (John 1:1, 14). The Bible's claim is *not* that Jesus was some sort of hybrid being who was part man and part God, or a divine/spiritual being who only *seemed* to have a body or who only inhabited a physical body temporarily. Rather, the Bible claims that in Jesus we see full humanity and full deity, two distinct natures in one person forever.

A primary way Jesus is shown to be divine in Scripture is through demonstrations of his great power. But the Bible presents Jesus as divine in a variety of other ways as well:

His Own Words and Actions

- **He claimed to be eternal.** "'Very truly I tell you,' Jesus answered, 'before Abraham was born, I am!'" (John 8:58).
- **He claimed oneness with God** (John 10:30). For the record, the religious elite found this statement so shocking and blasphemous, they wanted to stone Jesus on the spot.
- **He accepted worship.** Following his resurrection, Jesus revealed himself to "doubting Thomas." "Thomas said to him, 'My Lord and my God!' Then Jesus told him, 'Because you have seen me, you have believed; blessed are those who have not seen and yet have believed'" (John 20:28–29). We also see this in Revelation 19:10, where an angel tells John not to bow down to worship him, for only Jesus is worthy of worship.

The Testimony of Others

- **He is described as the cosmic glue that holds the universe together.** "He is before all things, and in him all things hold together" (Colossians 1:17).
- **He is described as all-knowing.** "In [Christ] are hidden all the treasures of wisdom and knowledge" (Colossians 2:3).
- **He is said to be present everywhere.** "Christ is all, and is in all" (Colossians 3:11).
- **His followers called him God.** "Our God and Savior Jesus Christ" (2 Peter 1:1).

In the face of such claims, we are left with three possibilities: Jesus was knowingly lying (and therefore evil—not the good teacher so many make him out to be), he was unknowingly deluded (i.e., crazy), or he was telling the truth (in which case we should respond to him as Thomas did).

IS JESUS REALLY GOD?

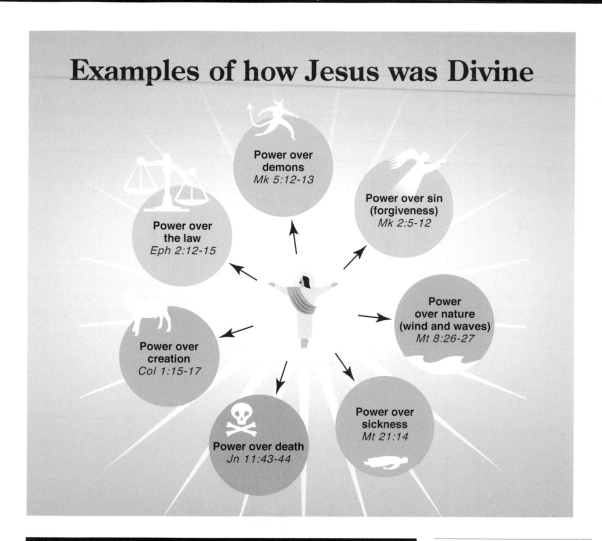

Examples of how Jesus was Divine

Power over demons
Mk 5:12-13

Power over sin (forgiveness)
Mk 2:5-12

Power over the law
Eph 2:12-15

Power over nature (wind and waves)
Mt 8:26-27

Power over creation
Col 1:15-17

Power over sickness
Mt 21:14

Power over death
Jn 11:43-44

Life Application

Which of the biblical arguments for the deity (divinity) of Christ do you find most compelling? How is your faith affected by the thought that had you lived in Galilee in, say, AD 25, you could have visited a carpenter's shop in Nazareth and looked directly into the eyes of the Almighty?

CROSS-REFERENCES

Ephesians 1:22–23

Philippians 3:20–21

Titus 2:13

Hebrews 1:1–8

CHAPTER 10

The Old Testament prophets explicitly predicted events from the life of Jesus centuries before his birth—eerily accurate details about his birth, life, ministry, death, and resurrection.

What does *messianic* mean? *Messianic* means "of or related to the Messiah." This title comes from the Hebrew word meaning "anointed one." The Greek equivalent is *Christ*. The Old Testament frequently refers to a great prophet/priest/king who would one day bring to earth a never-ending kingdom of righteousness and peace. Isaiah (and other prophets) told of a coming one who would take on the roles of suffering servant (Isaiah 52–53) and powerful ruler (Isaiah 60–61). By the first century, most messianic hopes were for a political deliverer only. We should note that Jesus did accept the title of Messiah when others identified him as such (see Matthew 21:9; Mark 10:46–48).

Are all these fulfilled messianic prophecies a giant coincidence? Perhaps, some theorize, all this was a fluky thing. That seems logically possible, except for the fact that a few math whizzes have calculated the likelihood of one person fulfilling even just 48 of these 300 prophecies. Those odds come to one in 10^{157} (that's a 1 followed by 157 zeros). In other words, a person could win the lottery *multiple times* before pulling off this feat.

Could the fulfillment of the messianic prophecies have been the result of elaborate human planning? Maybe, some speculate, Jesus was just well-versed in Bible prophecies, and he purposely orchestrated his life events to make himself *appear* to be the one spoken of in all these Old Testament passages. For example, Jesus knew that Zechariah 9:9 speaks of Messiah riding a donkey, and that Isaiah 53:9 says the Lord's servant would be buried in a rich man's tomb. Consequently, the argument goes, Jesus could have arranged these events before the fact. The problem is, how do we explain all the prophesied events over which Jesus would have had no control, such as his place of birth or the actions of others toward him?

Life Application

In Luke 24:44, the resurrected Jesus told two of his followers that many things had been written about him in the Torah, the Prophets, and the Psalms. What is your favorite Old Testament passage that points to Christ?

CROSS-REFERENCES

Psalm 22

Luke 24:44

John 4:25–26

OLD TESTAMENT PROPHECIES JESUS FULFILLED

Prophecies Jesus Fulfilled

Born in Bethlehem
Mic. 5:2
Lk 2:4–7

Betrayed for 30 pieces of silver
Zec 11:12–13
Mt 26:14–16

Of the House of David
2Sa 7:12-13
Lk 1:32

Rides into Jerusalem on a donkey
Zec 9:9
Mt 21:1–3

Insulted by the crowd
Ps 22:6–8
Lk 23:35–36

His resurrection
Ps 16:9-10
Mt 28:6

Buried in a rich man's tomb
Isa 53:9
Mt 27:57-60

Called Immanuel
Isa 7:14
Mt 1:22–23

Betrayed by Judas
Ps 41:9
Mt 26:47–50

Soldiers cast lots for his clothing
Ps 22:18
Jn 19:23-24

Crucified with criminals
Isa 53:12
Lk 23:33

KEY

Old Testament Prophecy

New Testament Fulfillment

GETTING TO KNOW GOD

CHAPTER 11

For centuries Christians have wondered (and wrangled) over the nature of Jesus. One particular question—Was Jesus truly human?—has sparked heresies and heated church councils, plus more books and sermons than we could ever count.

Here, in brief, is what the New Testament reveals about the humanity of Jesus:

Jesus' early life. The Gospels tell of the birth of a Jewish boy in Bethlehem to low-income parents, Mary and Joseph. After living briefly in Egypt, this little family relocated to the Galilean village of Nazareth in northern Israel. There Joseph worked as a carpenter, and Jesus, the oldest of a growing brood, followed in the steps of his stepfather (Mark 6:3). Had you lived in the area at that time, you might have purchased a chair or plow handmade by Jesus.

Jesus' public ministry. Around the age of thirty, Jesus became an itinerant teacher. He gathered a band of followers and traveled about Israel announcing the kingdom of God. He did things that only God can do— heal the sick, calm storms, miraculously feed the hungry, raise the dead. But the Gospels also show him doing very *human* things— facing temptation (Matthew 4:1–11), walking along the beach (Matthew 4:18), attending weddings (John 2:1–12) and dinner parties (Matthew 9:10), carrying on conversations (John 3), napping (Mark 4:38), feeling weary (John 4:6)—even spitting (John 9:6) and sweating (Luke 22:44).

Jesus' death. At the end of his ministry, Jesus was arrested, bound, tried, and sentenced to death. Soldiers flogged him, spit on him, and punched him (Matthew 26:67). Then they nailed him to a cross. During this gruesome experience, Jesus bled, cried out, and admitted thirst (John 19:28). Eventually he stopped breathing (Mark 15:37). His followers then took his lifeless body and put it in a borrowed tomb on a Friday evening. By Sunday morning, Jesus was alive again. Before long he was preparing breakfast on the beach for his followers (John 21:12).

People are free to form whatever conclusions they wish about Jesus. But there's no getting around this: The New Testament depicts him as a real man who knew the limitations and pains of human existence. (For more on Jesus' deity, see chapter 9, "Is Jesus Really God?")

Life Application

What's harder for you to accept—the biblical claim that Jesus was and is fully *human*, or that he was and is fully *divine*? Take some time to ponder Hebrews 4:15 (a verse about why our Savior *had* to be human).

EXAMPLES OF JESUS' HUMANITY

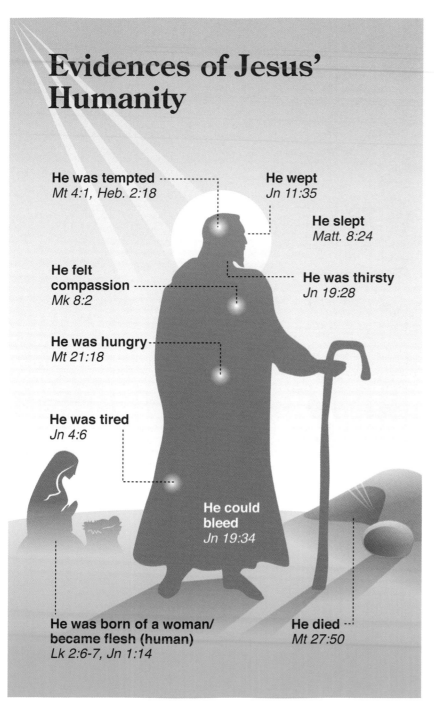

Evidences of Jesus' Humanity

He was tempted
Mt 4:1, Heb. 2:18

He wept
Jn 11:35

He slept
Matt. 8:24

He felt compassion
Mk 8:2

He was thirsty
Jn 19:28

He was hungry
Mt 21:18

He was tired
Jn 4:6

He could bleed
Jn 19:34

He was born of a woman/ became flesh (human)
Lk 2:6-7, Jn 1:14

He died
Mt 27:50

CROSS-REFERENCES

Mark 15:39

Luke 24:37–43

John 8:40

1 Timothy 2:5

CHAPTER 12

If God is in control of the world, and if he already knows all things, why should we bother to pray? To be sure, prayer is one of the greatest mysteries of the spiritual life. And yet there is no getting around the fact that God commands us to pray.

Prayer primarily involves two parts: first, the recognition of who God is and the acknowledgment of what he can do; and second, petitions of the one praying, whether they be for blessings, forgiveness, personal needs, or the needs of others. Ultimately, prayer deepens our personal dependence on God and our faith in him.

Multiple Scripture passages provide guidelines and reminders for prayer:

- **Pray with faith.** "Therefore I tell you, whatever you ask for in prayer, believe that you have received it, and it will be yours" (Mark 11:24).
- **Pray relentlessly** (Luke 18:1).
- **Pray in the name of Christ** (i.e., the kinds of prayers Jesus would pray; see John 14:13).
- **Pray in community (Acts 2:42).**
- **Pray with reliance on the Spirit.** "In the same way, the Spirit helps us in our weakness. We do not know what we ought to pray for, but the Spirit himself intercedes for us through groans that words cannot express" (Romans 8:26).
- **Pray continually** (1 Thessalonians 5:17).
- **Pray boldly** (Hebrews 4:16).
- **Pray in accordance with the will of God** (1 John 5:14–15). This is why one can never go wrong "praying Scripture."

Prayer is a genuine mystery. Although God knows our needs, he asks us to bring them to him in prayer. He can "move mountains," and he often does so in response to our requests.

We read in the Bible (and can verify from our own experience) that God works in mighty ways when we pray. When we pray earnestly, relentlessly, and dependently, we have the opportunity to enjoy seeing God do incredible work.

Life Application

Pray until you can pray; pray to be helped to pray and do not give up praying because you cannot pray. For . . . when you think you cannot pray, that is when you are praying.

Charles Spurgeon

CROSS-REFERENCES

Proverbs 15:8

Ephesians 6:18

Colossians 4:2

James 5:16

PRAYER: THE CHANNEL TO GOD

What Is Prayer?

The sacrifice of Jesus Christ has made a true and meaningful connection with God possible for everyone. God invites the followers of Christ to boldly approach him with their praises, thoughts, needs, hurts, hopes, and requests.

PURPOSE OF PRAYER
■ Worship God for who he is and thank him for what he's done
■ Cultivate a personal relationship with God
■ Reflect on daily actions
■ Make requests and ask for guidance
■ Express faith in God
■ Repent and receive forgiveness
Eph 1:5–6,11–12; 3:12; Heb 10:19–22

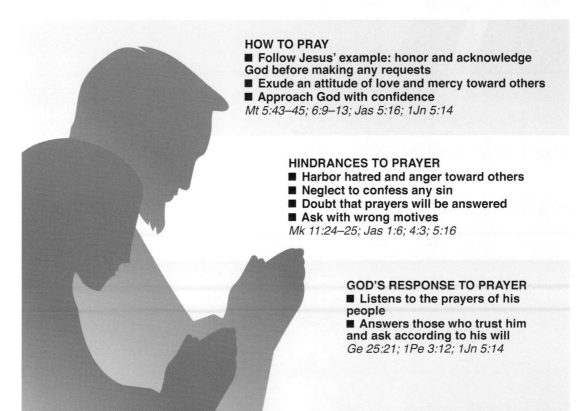

HOW TO PRAY
■ Follow Jesus' example: honor and acknowledge God before making any requests
■ Exude an attitude of love and mercy toward others
■ Approach God with confidence
Mt 5:43–45; 6:9–13; Jas 5:16; 1Jn 5:14

HINDRANCES TO PRAYER
■ Harbor hatred and anger toward others
■ Neglect to confess any sin
■ Doubt that prayers will be answered
■ Ask with wrong motives
Mk 11:24–25; Jas 1:6; 4:3; 5:16

GOD'S RESPONSE TO PRAYER
■ Listens to the prayers of his people
■ Answers those who trust him and ask according to his will
Ge 25:21; 1Pe 3:12; 1Jn 5:14

CHAPTER 13

Recited weekly in church services and whispered daily in private devotions by Catholics, Protestants, and Orthodox believers alike, the Lord's Prayer (Matthew 6:9–13; Luke 11:2–4) is surely the most frequently prayed prayer in human history. Why is this short spiritual supplication so beloved by so many?

The model. Jesus offered this petition as a "sample prayer." He meant, Pray along these lines—talk to God about these sorts of things. He surely didn't intend for his followers to merely repeat the words superstitiously, as though they were some kind of magical incantation. How do we know this? Because immediately before suggesting this rough outline for prayer, he discouraged all forms of robotic, mindless, repetitive praying (Matthew 6:7).

At first glance, we see his model is divided into two parts: (1) prayers that acknowledge God and his position and (2) prayers for ourselves (see image). But this model prayer offers more than just this simple division.

The scope. The prayer Jesus offered was all-encompassing. It highlights *God's nature* (he's our "Father in heaven"), and it seeks *God's glory* above all else ("hallowed be your name"). It then requests that *God's kingdom* (i.e., his righteous reign) might come and *God's will* be done on the earth. Finally,

it expresses dependence on *God's provision* ("daily bread"), *God's mercy* ("forgive us"), and *God's protection* ("lead us not into temptation, but deliver us").

The balance. Unlike so many prayers that tend to be either divorced from real life or utterly self-absorbed, Jesus' model prayer begins with a healthy reminder that God's reputation and agenda are paramount—not ours. We exist for him—not the other way around. The prayer ends with reminders that we can trust God to meet our material and spiritual needs as we seek to live for him and his glory.

Life Application

Personalizing the Lord's Prayer might look something like this:

Father in heaven, I want to honor you today. Please reign in my life—so that my thoughts, words, actions, interactions, and deeds help bring about your will at home, at work, and in all my relationships. I trust you will meet my material needs. I thank you for the forgiveness that is mine in Christ. Give me strength and wisdom today to say no to sin and yes to your Spirit. Amen.

WHAT'S SO GREAT ABOUT THE LORD'S PRAYER?

Elements of the Lord's Prayer

FOR GOD

May your name be honored as holy *Mt 6:9; Lk 11:2*

May your kingdom come *Mt 6:10; Lk 11:2*

May your will be done on earth as in heaven *Mt 6:10*

FOR US

Give us our bread each day *Mt 6:11; Lk 11:3*

Forgive us as we forgive others *Mt 6:12; Lk 11:4*

Keep us from temptation and evil *Mt 6:13; Lk 11:4*

CROSS-REFERENCES

Luke 11:5–13

Ephesians 1:15–23

1 Thessalonians 5:17

1 John 5:14–15

PART 2

LIVING IN OUR WORLD

CHAPTER 14

Whether it's researchers looking through telescopes and microscopes or "regular people" gawking at breathtaking mountain or ocean views, the question is always the same: *Where did all this come from? Did it just happen?*

It's the question of origins. Over the centuries, civilizations, scientists, philosophers, and theologians have proposed a number of ways to explain the existence of the world we see—and all the mysteries we can't see. What are these primary worldviews?

Atheism is the view that rejects the very idea of God. Atheism says that the cosmos is, in the famous words of scientist Carl Sagan, "all that is or was or ever will be." Why resort to primitive spiritual beliefs, atheists ask, when the universe—and everything in it—can be explained materialistically, scientifically, rationally? They conclude that the world we see came into existence randomly, by chance. There is no intelligent cause behind or beyond the material world.

Polytheism is the primitive belief (think: the Old Testament Canaanites or ancient Greeks) in multiple finite gods who are thought to be active in the world. These gods are seen as having power over limited spheres—for example, they bring (or withhold) blessings like rain or fertility.

Deism proposes a supreme being (usually impersonal) who created the universe but then withdrew, leaving the world to run on strictly naturalistic principles. Miracles? Some deists like Thomas Jefferson and Voltaire insisted there's no such thing.

Pantheism is the (typically Eastern) worldview that sees only one ultimate reality: God. In other words, God is all and in all. Everything is God—the universe and everything in it. Buddhism and Hinduism hold this view (although Hinduism is also polytheistic). Even a handful of environmentalists are somewhat pantheistic in their reverence for nature.

While acknowledging that people embrace these various ideas, the Bible advocates *theism*. A perspective shared broadly by Jews, Christians, and Muslims, theism is the view that an infinite all-powerful God made the finite, material universe out of nothing. What's more, theists see God sustaining the world and remaining active in human affairs. The Bible concludes with apocalyptic imagery of God destroying the present cosmos (2 Peter 3:10–12) and then establishing "a new heaven and a new earth" (Revelation 21–22).

GOD'S INTERACTION WITH THE WORLD

God's Response to the World

He populated it
Ge 1:26

He will judge it
Dt 32:22

He created it
Ge 1:1

He controls it
Ps 135:6-7

He loves it
Jn 3:16

He owns it
Ps 24:1

He sustains it
Job 5:10

He will destroy it
2Pe 3:10

He will create it anew
Isa 65:17

Life Application

Theism says that God is active in this world that he made and loves and is making new. Where do you see God active in *your* life? Where do you *need* to see God at work in a powerful way?

CROSS-REFERENCES

Psalm 9:8

Isaiah 13:11

Jeremiah 10:12

CHAPTER 15

Humans are shortsighted. We see the marvels of creation and ooh and aah. But too often we stop there. We get so enthralled with these gifts that we forget to trace them back to their source—the even more amazing Giver responsible for them.

When Jesus began his public ministry, he routinely seized upon objects from the natural world to illustrate spiritual truth. He said people were like skittish, helpless sheep (Matthew 9:36). He said the Holy Spirit of God is like the wind (John 3:8). A dead bird prompted a comment about God's all-knowing nature (Matthew 10:29). He used seeds and various kinds of soil to point out the different ways people respond to God's truth (Luke 8:4–15). He once cursed a fig tree for falsely giving the appearance of fruitfulness (Mark 11:12–14).

This comparing of the physical and spiritual is common throughout the Bible. The passages that liken an attribute of God to something in nature are usually intended to suggest one or more of the following:

God's Attributes Compared to Nature
Psalm 36:5–6

God's love...
Is higher than the heavens
Ps 108:4

God's righteousness...
Reaches to the heavens
Ps 71:19

God's name endures forever...
And continues as long as the sun.
Ps 72:17

God's faithfulness...
Reaches to the skies
Ps 36:5; Ps 57:10;
Ps 108:4

God's love...
Reaches to the heavens
Ps 36:5; Ps 57:10

For as high as the heavens are above the earth...
So great is his love for those who fear him
Ps 103:11

As the heavens are higher than the earth...
So are God's ways higher than our ways and
his thoughts than our thoughts.
Isa 55:9

God's righteousness...
Is like the highest mountains
Ps 36:6

God's justice...
Is like the great deep
Ps 36:6

UNDERSTANDING GOD'S ATTRIBUTES THROUGH NATURE

The infinity of God. When we look up wordlessly at the Milky Way or stare out breathlessly at the ocean, we feel small and vulnerable—because we are. The biblical writers mean for us in such moments to picture an endless supply of divine love, righteousness, and justice filling all that vastness. Staring at a massive mountain peak—all that ancient substance and permanence—we are to think of the One who existed before anything else. The words of Psalm 8:3–5 capture our experience well: "When I consider your heavens, the work of your fingers, the moon and the stars, which you have set in place, what is mankind that you are mindful of them, human beings that you care for them? You have made them a little lower than the angels and crowned them with glory and honor."

The mystery of God. So much about our world and universe is wild and unexplored. Almost every week researchers stumble upon some new species or never-before-seen wonder. The biblical writers want us to grasp that what is true in the natural world is even truer in the supernatural: "Can you fathom the mysteries of God?" (Job 11:7).

The beauty of God. The western sky ablaze at sunset. Waves crashing on the seashore at dawn. Majestic, snow-covered peaks against an azure sky. These heart-piercing sights are meant to remind us that God himself is beautiful beyond description: "One thing I ask from the LORD. . . to gaze on the beauty of the LORD and to seek him in his temple" (Psalm 27:4).

Let the natural point you to the supernatural, as indicated in Romans 1:20: "For since the creation of the world God's invisible qualities—his eternal power and divine nature—have been clearly seen, being understood from what has been made, so that people are without excuse."

Life Application

Psalm 46 speaks, not of natural delights, but of a natural disaster—of mountains crashing violently into the sea. Here we see the terror of creation in chaos, a devastating earthquake or landslide. In such earthshaking situations, the psalmist wants us to know that "God is our refuge and strength, an ever-present help in trouble" (Psalm 46:1). Consequently, we need not fear.

The message of the Bible is that nature, whether beautiful or terrible, can always turn our thoughts and hearts to God.

CROSS-REFERENCES

Job 12:7–10; 37:14–16

Psalm 104:24–25

John 1:3

CHAPTER 16

Travelers who have had the great privilege of gawking at the northern lights or standing breathlessly at the Grand Canyon have difficulty finding words to describe their experiences. We do indeed inhabit an amazing and wondrous creation—because we have an awesome Creator. It's not surprising that the Bible is filled with vivid imagery of how God made and sees the world.

Most of the biblical descriptions of how God crafted and cares for our world are meant to be more poetic than scientific. But just because the Bible's revelations about nature don't read like a doctoral student's dissertation on some aspect of biochemistry doesn't mean they can't teach us invaluable lessons. Here are three takeaways:

God is big. The imagery of God cupping the Pacific Ocean in his hand or "palming" the universe like an NBA star palms a basketball (Isaiah 40:12) is meant to convey one crucial truth: God is immense. Infinite. Large and in charge. This is especially helpful when life's problems seem overwhelming. God is big enough to engage our biggest troubles.

God is wise. The Bible's multiple "meteorological" references—to wind (Numbers 11:31), rain (Matthew 7:25), lightning (Psalm 18:14), mist (Genesis 2:6), dew (Proverbs 3:20), heat (Genesis 18:1), and cold (Job 37:9)—serve to remind us that our Creator has placed us in a remarkable ecosystem perfectly designed to sustain life and instill wonder.

God is kind. Preaching at Lystra to people who did not know the one true God, the apostle Paul declared, "Yet he has not left himself without testimony: He has shown kindness by giving you rain from heaven and crops in their seasons; he provides you with plenty of food and fills your hearts with joy" (Acts 14:17).

As you read Scripture and encounter passages that speak creatively of God's active involvement in making our world (and keeping it spinning), let your heart be filled with thankfulness and awe.

Life Application

Perhaps staring at a gorgeous sunset or a starry night sky, the prophet Jeremiah prayed, "Ah, Sovereign LORD, you have made the heavens and the earth by your great power and outstretched arm. Nothing is too hard for you" (Jeremiah 32:17).

Let the intricacy and beauty of nature move you in a similar way—to remember that the God you serve is a God who is able to do anything.

THE AWESOME CREATOR BEHIND OUR AMAZING CREATION

God's Explanation of Creation to Job

Job

He stretched a
measuring line
across it
38:5

He marked off
its dimensions
38:5

He clothed the
seas with clouds
38:9

He regulates the
dawning of the sun
38:12-13

He shut up the seas
behind doors
38:8

He fixed the limits
of the waves
38:10-11

He laid the earth's foundation
38:4

CROSS-REFERENCES

Psalm 69:34

Ecclesiastes 11:5

Mark 4:28

CHAPTER 17

What's going on in the natural world? The scientific community warns about dwindling honeybee populations and clean water supplies, as well as rising global temperatures and ocean levels. Almost daily we read about another earthquake, sinkhole, flood, approaching asteroid, wildfire, or Category 5 hurricane.

The Bible teaches these truths about our world:

God made the world (and autographed his work). Again and again, the Bible declares that God made the world from nothing (Genesis 1:1; Hebrews 11:3). In the same way that each Van Gogh original reveals the one-of-a-kind talent of the artist, so our intricate universe continually announces, "God made me." We see glimpses of the Creator's power, glory, and majesty in all that he has created (Psalm 19:1–2; Romans 1:20).

God entrusted the world to humanity. The plan of God involved commissioning humans to be the caretakers of his creation. The specific assignment? To rule or have dominion over every created thing (Genesis 1:28) and, in the idyllic paradise known as the garden of Eden, "to work it and take care of it" (i.e., to watch over it, to guard and protect it; Genesis 2:15).

God's world became the object of a curse. The Bible says that because of Adam and Eve's rebellion in Eden, the whole world fell under a curse (Genesis 3:1–19). Paul wrote of how this corruption of creation causes the world to groan (Romans 8:19–22).

God will one day reveal a new creation. The gospel says that God sent his Son into the world to deal fully and finally with sin and to remove every vestige of the curse (Revelation 22:3). Now, because of Jesus Christ's perfect life, sacrificial death, and glorious resurrection, believers can look forward to the day when all things will be made new (Revelation 21:5).

When have you seen the majesty of God in nature?

Life Application

Spend a few minutes carefully reading and meditating on Psalm 148. Why does the psalmist call on the stars and snow (and all sorts of other created things) to praise the Lord? How could you be a better steward of the world God has entrusted to your care?

CROSS-REFERENCES
Psalms 24:1; 65:5–13
Isaiah 40:12
Revelation 11:18

HOW NATURE REVEALS GOD

What the Bible Says About
Finding God in Nature
Psalm 19:1–2; Romans 1:18–20

The heavens declare
the glory of God
Ps 19:1

God sends rain & snow
Jer 14:22, Job 5:10, Job 37:6

God controls the weather
(lightning, wind, rain)
Ps 135:7

God covers the
sky with clouds
Ps 147:8

The heavens, moon
& stars are the work
of God's fingers
Ps 8:3

The skies proclaim the
work of his hands
Ps 19:1

Heavens & skies reveal
knowledge of God
Ps 19:2

Heavens & skies
speak about God
Ps 19:2

God has set His glory
in the heavens
Ps 8:1

The heavens proclaim
his righteousness
Ps 50:6

God made
plants & trees
Ge 1:11-12

Creation reveals
God's power &
divine nature
Ro 1:20

God made
animals/fish/birds
Ge 1:21 & 25

PART 3

MARRIAGE
AND FAMILY

CHAPTER 18

In the early days of ultrasound imaging, pregnant couples often had to use their imagination:

> **Technician:** Look! There's his arm and his little nose and mouth. Isn't that amazing?
>
> **Expectant father:** (*Scratching his head.*) If you say so.

Now, however, with the advent of 3D and even 4D ultrasound machines, views inside the womb are vivid and breathtaking. What does the Bible say about these tiny, fast-developing humans?

- God's original design was for families (Genesis 1:28)—parents being fruitful and multiplying (i.e., having babies).
- Children are described as a *heritage* and a *reward* (Psalm 127:3–5).
- Not being able to have children is a source of great heartache for many couples, both now and in Bible times (see Sarai in Genesis 11:30 and Hannah in 1 Samuel 1:10).
- Pregnancy is a cause for great joy and celebration (Psalm 113:9).
- Unborn babies can feel and express emotion. "As soon as the sound of your greeting reached my ears, the baby in my womb leaped for joy" (Luke 1:44).
- God has unique plans for every child in every womb (Jeremiah 1:5; Galatians 1:15).
- Childbirth wasn't originally intended to be painful (Genesis 3:14–16; John 16:21). It's only because of sin that labor and delivery became unpleasant.
- It's good to dedicate our children—that is, give them back to God (1 Samuel 1:21–28; Luke 2:22).
- Grandchildren are a source of great delight (Proverbs 17:6).
- God's plan for saving the world involved a newborn baby (Isaiah 7:14; Luke 2:6–7).

Life Application

Jesus had a lot to say about babies and children. He implied that little children have guardian angels (Matthew 18:10). He often took children in his arms (Mark 9:36–37) and blessed them (Mark 10:13–16). And when he heard some of his disciples discouraging parents from "bothering" Jesus with their infants and small kids (Luke 18:15–17), he chastised them, saying, "Let the little children come to me, and do not hinder them, for the kingdom of heaven belongs to such as these" (Matthew 19:14).

A BABY AS GOD'S GIFT

Just a Fetus?

What Psalms says about unborn children

Designed and formed by God
139:13–14

Seen and known by God
22:10; 139:15–16

Sinful from conception
51:5; 58:3

Acknowledged and valued
22:30–31; 78:6; 102:18

Given wisdom from God
51:6

Brought out of the womb by God
22:9; 71:6

CROSS-REFERENCES

Genesis 25:21

Psalm 8:2

Ecclesiastes 11:5

CHAPTER 19

Everybody has opinions about marriage—what it is or what it should be.

The Bible discusses marriage before it mentions any other human institution. Many scholars believe the union of Adam and Eve—before sin entered the world—is meant to model God's perfect design for marriage. What does Adam and Eve's experience show marriage to be?

- **A source of companionship.** In the bliss of Eden, where Adam had unfettered access to God, the Almighty said, "It is not good for the man to be alone" (Genesis 2:18).
- **A valuable partnership.** "I will make a helper suitable for him" (Genesis 2:18). Far from a derogatory term, "helper" is often used of God in the Bible (Psalms 33:20; 115:9). If anything, rather than demeaning Eve, the word suggests limitations in Adam. "Suitable" means "corresponding to," and suggests a perfect fit.
- **A new entity.** "A man leaves his father and mother" (Genesis 2:24). Biblically speaking, each marriage is the launching of a distinctly new family unit.
- **A unique union.** The Bible speaks of marriage as a heterosexual, monogamous relationship. In Genesis 1:27 we read that God "created mankind in his own image . . . male and female he created them" (the implication is that the different sexes are required to properly image God / reflect his nature). In the next chapter's description and discussion of marriage, we read, "That is why a man . . . is united to his wife" (Genesis 2:24). Notice that this prototypical marriage relationship is comprised of "a man" and "his wife" (singular). Two individuals—and no more—and two different genders—not one. The Hebrew word translated "united" here means "clinging or sticking to." The idea is one of commitment; no one is going anywhere.
- **A selfless, intimate relationship.** "They become one flesh. Adam and his wife were both naked, and they felt no shame" (Genesis 2:24–25). The first couple—before the fall—experienced the safety, trust, and joy of being so focused on one another that they felt no need to cover up emotionally or physically.

From the days of Adam and Eve, God outlined marriage as a permanent relationship between a man and woman that offers a completeness and companionship that cannot be found anywhere else.

THE BIBLE ON MARRIAGE

Guidelines for Marriage

DO'S	DONT'S
Remain faithful to your spouse Ex 20:14	**Don't covet another person's spouse** Ex 20:17
Stay married 1Co 7:10-11	**Do not marry a close relative** Lev 20:17
Marry someone with similar religious belief & commitment 2Co 6:14-15	**Do not allow relatives to intrude upon the marriage** Ge 2:24

OTHER GUIDELINES

Those of the opposite sex were made for each other Mt 19:4–6

Not everyone was made to be married 1Co 7:8-9

If you married an unbeliever, stay with them if they are willing 1Co 7:12-16

Life Application

Which of the following are good, biblical reasons for marrying, and which are suspect ones?

- to better glorify and serve God
- to give the world a vivid picture of Christ's love for the church
- to avoid sexual immorality
- so I can be taken care of
- to save on my bills and expenses
- because I'm lonely
- because I'm not getting any younger
- because all my friends are tying the knot
- to have kids/a family
- because I can't imagine life without my sweetheart
- to become the person God means for me to be
- to find a soul mate and partner in life

CROSS-REFERENCES

Genesis 29:15–30

Mark 10:2–12

Ephesians 5:21–33

CHAPTER 20

On Saturday a lovestruck couple pays big bucks to dress up, recite marriage vows, and celebrate with family and friends. On Monday another (disillusioned) couple pays big bucks so that a couple of divorce attorneys can help dissolve their union.

Why do so many couples have so much trouble making marriage work? What biblical insights can help husbands and wives build healthier, happier marriages?

The most extensive New Testament passage on marriage is found in Ephesians 5. We could summarize its teaching this way:

Each Spouse

"Be very careful" (v. 15). Marriage is tricky. We can't even understand our own hearts, much less another person's. Proceed with caution.

"Be filled with the Spirit" (v. 18). Think of how much marital misery could be avoided if husbands and wives allowed the Holy Spirit of the living God to reign in them—and rein them in. (In truth, it's hard to see how any of the commands that follow could be obeyed apart from such supernatural help.)

"Submit to one another" (v. 21). Submission is voluntary subordination. Imagine the trust in a marriage in which both husband and wife are constantly and selflessly deferring to the needs and desires of the other.

Wives

"Submit" (v. 22). A wife has far less trouble with this command—and with the additional command to "respect [your] husband" (v. 33)—when the husband faithfully carries out his role, which is as follows.

Husbands

"Love your wives, just as Christ loved the church" (v. 25). It's a staggering command, and it prompts the question: How did Christ show his love for the church? He *died* for his church. His love was (and is) sacrificial, total, unconditional, faithful, and undying. God did not design marriage to be a sexist, male-dominated institution. On the contrary, husbands are called to love their wives with ultimate love and sacrifice.

When each spouse is willing to sacrifice and to suspend their interests for their spouse, we find a model of love and humility that imitates Christ.

Life Application

Informally interview some married couples. Ask them two questions: (1) What's the best marital counsel you've ever received? (2) What two bits of wisdom do you wish you had known when you first married?

THE "HIS" AND "HERS" OF MARRIAGE

Role of Husbands and Wives

Husband's Role

Wife's Role

Respect your husband
Eph 5:33

Love your wife
Eph 5:25; Col 3:19

Submit to your husband
Eph 5:22; Col 3:18

Leave parents and unite with your wife
Ge 2:24; Eph 5:31

Be self-controlled, pure, productive, and kind
Titus 2:5

Shared Roles

Love your husband
Titus 2:4

Be considerate to your wife
1Pe 3:7

Fulfill your sexual obligation
1Co 7:2-4

Be faithful to your husband
1Ti 5:9

Remain married
1Co 7:10-11

Be a helper to your husband
Ge 2:18

Be faithful to your wife
1Ti 3:2; Titus 1:6

Win your husband over with your behavior rather than words
1Pe 3:1-2

Treat your wife with respect
1Pe 3:7

Have beauty that comes from within rather than from without
1Pe 3:3-4

CROSS-REFERENCES

Psalm 128

Proverbs 5:15–20; 19:14

Matthew 5:31–32

CHAPTER 21

Because the Bible is the product of ancient, male-dominated cultures, the majority of its "heroes" are men (think Abraham, Moses, David, Peter, and Paul). Even so, it's not at all the sexist, misogynistic book that many claim. Women like Sarah, Rebekah, Rahab, Deborah, Ruth, Esther—plus a parade of New Testament Marys—are featured prominently with great honor.

Far from denigrating women, the Bible is revolutionary for the way it elevates women. Proverbs 31, for example, paints a picture of how an excellent wife can make a remarkable difference in her home and culture.

Life Application

If you've had the blessing of being reared by a godly mother or grandmother, or if you've been graced to be married to a woman of God, take some time right now to pause and thank the Lord. Then take a few minutes to write a note of appreciation. This exercise will cause your heart to swell with gratitude. More importantly, it will bring great encouragement to the one who prompted your note.

Note the traits of this "wonder woman":

- Has "noble character" (v. 10). The weaker sex? Hardly. This phrase conveys the idea of strength and capability.
- Is "worth far more than rubies" (v. 10). This poetic illustration shows the great value the Bible ascribes to women.
- Is trustworthy (v. 11) because of her proven character (v. 12).
- Is described as industrious (vv. 13–14, 27) and hardworking (v. 15).
- Is an able administrator (v. 15) with a savvy business mind (v. 16). In ancient cultures women weren't allowed to buy and sell property. The remarkable woman described here, however, was breaking through glass ceilings long before that phrase was coined.
- Is tireless (vv. 17–19).
- Is compassionate (v. 20).
- Is proactive, forward-thinking, and prepared (vv. 21–25).
- Is creative (v. 24) and talented.
- Is widely respected (v. 25), appreciated, and praised (vv. 28–30).
- Is wise and kind (v. 26).
- Is God-fearing (v. 30).

What woman or girl wouldn't want to be described in these ways? What man wouldn't want a wife who fit this description?

PROVERBS 31: A WORD FOR WOMEN

And while Proverbs 31 reveals qualities of a noble wife, the characteristics listed in this famous chapter are not limited to those who are married. While these traits can be beneficial in a marriage relationship, they are timeless and applicable in any context.

CROSS-REFERENCES

Proverbs 11:16; 14:1; 21:19

1 Timothy 3:11

1 Peter 3:1–2

MARRIAGE & FAMILY

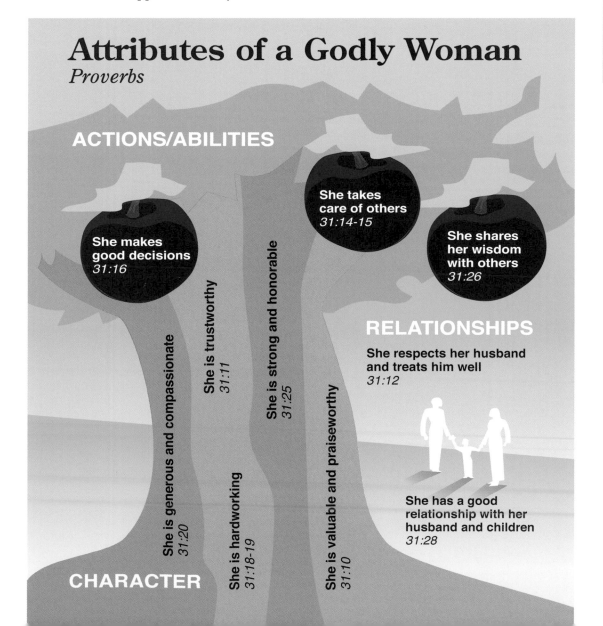

Attributes of a Godly Woman
Proverbs

ACTIONS/ABILITIES

She makes good decisions
31:16

She takes care of others
31:14-15

She shares her wisdom with others
31:26

RELATIONSHIPS

She respects her husband and treats him well
31:12

She has a good relationship with her husband and children
31:28

She is generous and compassionate
31:20

She is trustworthy
31:11

She is hardworking
31:18-19

She is strong and honorable
31:25

She is valuable and praiseworthy
31:10

CHARACTER

CHAPTER 22

Someone once likened parenting to walking around with your heart outside your body. Birthing or adopting a child is scary and gratifying, exasperating and exhilarating all at once. Leaving the hospital, you are hit with the reality that you're completely responsible for a tiny, helpless new person. You have a few vague, untested parenting theories, maybe, and a whole host of unspoken fears. What to do? What does the Bible say?

Before you dive into the daily practicalities of parenting a child, it's good to remember some foundational truths about the heavenly Father who parents *you*. These biblical truths can calm the anxious heart of any mom, the reeling mind of every dad:

God's love and goodness. You know that inexpressible, fierce love you have for your baby? The Bible says that God's love for your child is infinitely deeper, higher, and wider (Psalm 36:5). All the good things you desire for your child pale compared to the perfect things God wants for him or her. "If you, then, though you are evil, know how to give good gifts to your children, how much more will your Father in heaven give good gifts to those who ask him!" (Matthew 7:11).

God's control and power. Every parent wants to pull strings and orchestrate events so that his or her child enjoys every conceivable advantage. Here's the truth: God is in charge of outcomes. The Bible speaks repeatedly of God's grip on all things—he never "loses control" of situations (Deuteronomy 4:39; 1 Chronicles 29:12; Psalm 47:2). What's more, "nothing is too hard" for him (Jeremiah 32:17). This means that you don't have to be a control freak. You can rest in these reassuring realities.

God's knowledge and wisdom. When you've run out of parenting tricks and you're clueless about what to do next, God has an infinite supply of wise insight and brilliant counsel for you (John 16:13; James 1:5). His Word (2 Timothy 3:16–17), his people (1 Thessalonians 5:11), and his Spirit will guide you (Galatians 5:16) as you navigate the thrills, chills, and spills of parenting.

Life Application

Two realities every parent should recognize? (1) Children are natural mimics. (2) More is caught than taught. No wonder J. C. Ryle admonished, "Fathers and mothers, do not forget that children learn more by the eye than they do by the ear. . . . What they see has a much stronger effect on their minds than what they are told."

WISDOM FOR PARENTS

Biblical Guidelines for Parents

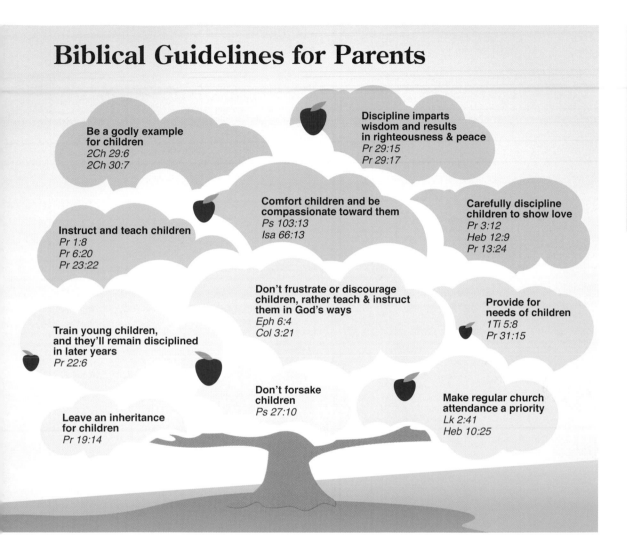

Be a godly example for children
2Ch 29:6
2Ch 30:7

Discipline imparts wisdom and results in righteousness & peace
Pr 29:15
Pr 29:17

Comfort children and be compassionate toward them
Ps 103:13
Isa 66:13

Carefully discipline children to show love
Pr 3:12
Heb 12:9
Pr 13:24

Instruct and teach children
Pr 1:8
Pr 6:20
Pr 23:22

Don't frustrate or discourage children, rather teach & instruct them in God's ways
Eph 6:4
Col 3:21

Provide for needs of children
1Ti 5:8
Pr 31:15

Train young children, and they'll remain disciplined in later years
Pr 22:6

Don't forsake children
Ps 27:10

Make regular church attendance a priority
Lk 2:41
Heb 10:25

Leave an inheritance for children
Pr 19:14

CROSS-REFERENCES

Deuteronomy 6:1–9

1 Kings 1:5–6

Proverbs 17:21

PART 4

FRIENDS, NEIGHBORS, AND ENEMIES

CHAPTER 23

They had always thought of themselves as Jesus' *disciples* (i.e., his student-apprentices). And on many occasions they functioned as his *helpers*. So imagine how surprised the Twelve must have felt when Jesus announced, "I no longer call you servants, because a servant does not know his master's business. Instead, I have called you *friends*, for everything that I learned from my Father I have made known to you" (John 15:15, emphasis added).

Friends of Jesus? There is no greater honor or blessing on earth. Jesus is the ultimate good friend.

Jesus possesses—perfectly—all the traits of a good friend. He . . .

Gives us flawless counsel. In fact, before he returned to heaven, he arranged to send his followers an indwelling Counselor and Helper—the Holy Spirit (John 14:16; 16:7).

Offered his life for us (John 10:15). Jesus' death paid for our sins while we were still sinners. His spotless life secured our righteousness.

Offers help and comfort when we're sick or scared. The Gospels show Christ as quick to come to the aid of those who hurt (Luke 4:40; John 14:27).

Doesn't leave loved ones behind when life gets hard. From the agony of the cross, for example, Jesus arranged for his friend John to take care of his mother, Mary (John 19:25–27).

Feels sympathetic and comforts us during difficulties. The Gospels reveal a compassionate Savior who assured his followers the blessing of divine comfort (Matthew 5:4).

Rejoices and mourns with us. John showed Jesus celebrating at a wedding (John 2:1–11) and weeping with grieving friends (John 11).

Is irate when those he loves are ignored or mistreated. Jesus often became furious with Israel's callous religious leaders, who used rather than served people (Mark 3:1–5; John 8:1–11).

Eagerly wants to see us succeed (Luke 10:17–24). Remember how excited Jesus was when his disciples returned full of joy over what they'd seen God do on their first "short-term mission trip"?

Never stops loving us. As he told his original followers on the eve of laying down his life, "As the Father has loved me, so have I loved you. Now remain in my love" (John 15:9).

Doesn't envy us. On the contrary, Jesus wants us to have everything good. He even made us his fellow heirs (Matthew 25:34).

By any standard of measure, Jesus isn't just a "good friend." He's the best friend we could ever have—one who went so far as to lay down his life for us (John 15:13).

FINDING (OR BEING) A GOOD FRIEND

Loving One Another

Love one another

Jn 13:34   1Jn 3:23
Jn 13:35   1Jn 4:7
Ro 13:8   1Jn 4:11
Heb 13:1   1Jn 4:12
1Pe 3:8   2Jn 5
1Jn 3:11

Encourage one another

2Co 13:11
1Th 4:18
1Th 5:11
Heb 3:13

Help each other during trials

Gal 6:2

Live in peace and harmony with one another

1Co 1:10
Ro 12:16
1Th 5:13

Serve each other without grumbling

Gal 5:13
Jn 13:14
1Pe 4:9

Be humble, compassionate and gentle with each other

Eph 4:2
1Pe 3:8
1Pe 5:5

Forgive and submit to one another

Eph 4:32
Col 3:13
Eph 5:21

Be devoted to one another, honor others, and do good to each other

Ro 12:10
1Th 5:15

Don't judge each other; rather accept one another

Ro 14:13
Ro 15:7

Speak kindly about and to each other

Jas 4:11
Jas 5:9

CROSS-REFERENCES

Exodus 33:11

Luke 5:33–35

John 21:1–14

CHAPTER 24

We live in the most "connected" generation ever—and perhaps the loneliest. People seem to have more and more online friends, but fewer and fewer "inlife" companions and confidants.

Why are meaningful friendships increasingly rare? And where can we find help in learning how to develop healthy real-life connections?

Proverbs and Ecclesiastes are classified as Old Testament wisdom literature. Most of the content of these books is ascribed to Solomon.

The Hebrew word translated "wisdom" is *hokmah*. It literally means "skill or expertise" and was commonly used to describe the handiwork of artisans who displayed rare ability in their craft. The biblical writers took this word and used it to refer broadly to the ability of some to skillfully navigate life. Biblically speaking, a wise person is adept or competent at handling everyday things like money, work, and human relationships.

What's interesting is that in the Bible (as in life) the relationships we've been given to wisely manage vary in their intimacy. For example, the Hebrew word *rea* can have various meanings, depending on the context. The word can refer to any of the following:

- **A countryman (group identity).** This is one who is of the same racial or social group (Exodus 2:13), a fellow citizen with whom one may not have a previous connection or personal history.
- **A neighbor (geographical proximity).** This is a person who lives nearby (Exodus 22:7), perhaps a casual acquaintance.
- **A friend (personal intimacy).** This is a trusted companion or comrade (Job 6:14), a person with whom one enjoys a close association.

Obviously, we are affected most by those to whom we are closest. Thus the heavy emphasis by Solomon on choosing close friends carefully and—when you find some choice ones—sticking together for the long haul.

Life Application

Think about your long history of friendship—childhood friends, high school buddies, college chums. Who are the people you stay in touch with on a casual basis? Who are your closest friends—who know you best and love you most? What relationship wisdom from Solomon do you most need to remember and apply today?

GOD'S WORD ON FRIENDSHIP

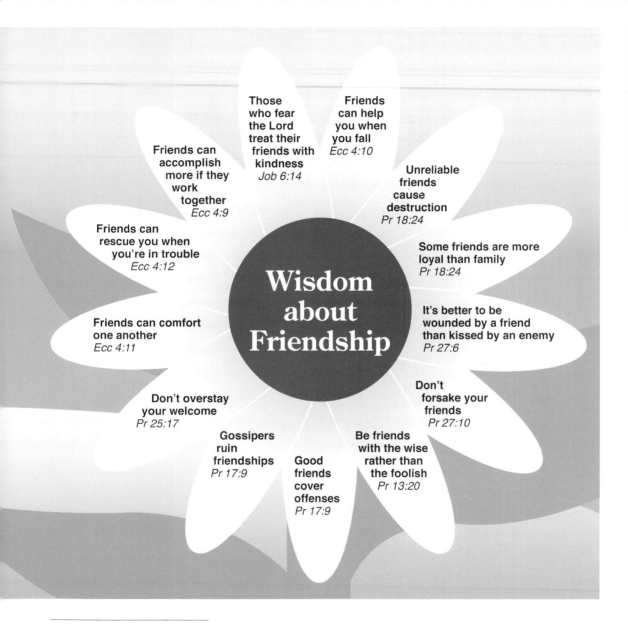

Wisdom about Friendship

Those who fear the Lord treat their friends with kindness
Job 6:14

Friends can help you when you fall
Ecc 4:10

Friends can accomplish more if they work together
Ecc 4:9

Unreliable friends cause destruction
Pr 18:24

Friends can rescue you when you're in trouble
Ecc 4:12

Some friends are more loyal than family
Pr 18:24

Friends can comfort one another
Ecc 4:11

It's better to be wounded by a friend than kissed by an enemy
Pr 27:6

Don't overstay your welcome
Pr 25:17

Don't forsake your friends
Pr 27:10

Gossipers ruin friendships
Pr 17:9

Good friends cover offenses
Pr 17:9

Be friends with the wise rather than the foolish
Pr 13:20

CROSS-REFERENCES

Exodus 33:11

Deuteronomy 13:6–8

1 Samuel 18:1

CHAPTER 25

Something seems amiss when we use the same word *love* to describe how we feel about our Maker, our mate, the movie we just saw, and the meal we're about to eat. But what is *real* love? God's love is the basis for our definition of love.

The Bible speaks of love as our defining characteristic. In John 13:34–35, Jesus said that love for one another—not our theological knowledge, nor our maintaining high moral standards—is the distinguishing mark of his followers. The world will know we are Christ's disciples by our *love*.

Here's what the Bible says about the whys and hows of loving one another:

Sacrificial. Love is a sacrifice. Love inevitably means giving (John 3:16)—our attention, time, energy, resources, valuables—even laying down our lives for others (John 15:13). A life of love will include allowing disruptions and inconvenience, swallowing pride, and surrendering personal agendas. Such an unselfish life is not natural—it's supernatural. We can't do it apart from Christ (John 15:5).

Selfless. Love seeks the best and works for the ultimate good of the other. Love has one unselfish goal—to see the other person become all that God wants him or her to be (Galatians 4:19; Ephesians 4:13; Philippians 2:4; Colossians 1:28–29).

Solid. Love is willing to say and do hard things. Many assume that love is mushy.

It is anything but. Real love tells the truth even when the truth is hard to hear. "Better is open rebuke than hidden love" (Proverbs 27:5; cf. Psalm 141:5). It even allows and/or administers "negative consequences" when such things will prove beneficial (Hebrews 12:6).

Love doesn't throw in the towel. So much of what passes for "love" is conditional—contingent on this or dependent on that. Such "love" is often short-lived. The love of Christians, however—which comes from God (1 John 4:7)—"always perseveres . . . never fails" (1 Corinthians 13:7–8).

Life Application

The renowned theologian Augustine of Hippo said, "What does love look like? It has the hands to help others. It has the feet to hasten to the poor and needy. It has eyes to see misery and want. It has the ears to hear the sighs and sorrows of men. That is what love looks like."

Using your hands, feet, eyes, and ears, how can you show love to someone today?

CROSS-REFERENCES

Proverbs 27:6

1 Corinthians 10:24; 13

LIFE TOGETHER

Traits of a Good Friend

G — Gives you good advice — Pr 27:9

O — Offers you help when you're sick or in need — Mk 2:3-4

O — Offers his/her life for you — Ro 16:3-4 — Jn 15:13

D — Doesn't leave you behind when life gets hard — Ru 1:16-17

F — Feels sympathetic and comforts you during difficulties — Job 2:11

R — Rejoices and mourns with you — Ro 12:15

I — Is irate when you're treated badly or unfairly — 1Sa 20:32-34

E — Eagerly wants to see you succeed — 1Ki 5:1

N — Never stops loving you — Pr 17:17

D — Doesn't envy you when you succeed — 1Sa 23:17

CHAPTER 26

We routinely send rockets and satellites into outer space. We've mapped the human genome and can manipulate human DNA. We have robots now that can perform brain surgery. Given all these advancements, why does the human race still have so many interpersonal difficulties?

Here (in brief) is how the Bible says we can improve our relationships:

Look back—be *retroactive*. If we have any sort of history with a neighbor, coworker, or acquaintance, that experience likely includes both positive and negative moments. Relationships are never improved by ignoring hurtful interactions or forgetting happy ones. It's only by humbly addressing the former (Matthew 5:23–25) and happily remembering the latter that we keep the peace and build ever-stronger bonds with others. The Bible encourages us to look back over our histories with others. Rough patches need to be smoothed over (Colossians 3:13). Good times ought to be celebrated.

Look ahead—be *proactive*. The famous "Golden Rule" (Matthew 7:12)—if rigorously practiced—would eliminate almost all our relational difficulties. Being empathetic—that is, being mindful of the needs, desires, and feelings of others—keeps us from having to come back later and apologize for thoughtless words and selfish actions.

Look around—be *reactive*. Love watches vigilantly, then responds quickly and decisively. Thus, when we become aware of relational needs or problems, we act immediately. In the case of unaddressed tension or unresolved conflict, the Bible is clear: "If it is possible, as far as it depends on you, live at peace with everyone" (Romans 12:18). This doesn't mean we will be able to resolve every disagreement perfectly, but it does mean that we need to do everything in our power to clear the air and keep the peace.

Life Application

Good interactions with others aren't dependent on having a certain temperament. You don't need a "big" outgoing personality. You can be a shy introvert and still enjoy great relationships. Each morning, pray for God's help in turning your gaze outward. Then pay attention to other people. Put yourself in their shoes. In God's strength, determine to serve them and treat them like Jesus would.

BUILDING STRONGER RELATIONSHIPS

Principles from Jesus about Dealing with Others

DO THIS

Do to others what you want them to do to you
Mt 7:12

Love one another
Jn 13:34–35

Love your enemies
Mt 5:44–45

Be forgiving
Mt 6:14–15

Give to those who ask anything of you
Mt 5:42

If anyone has something against you, be the first to make amends
Mt 5:23–24

Settle disputes before they get out of hand
Mt 5:25

Be good to others
Pr 3:27

DON'T DO THIS

Do not judge hypocritically
Mt 7:1–5

Don't retaliate
Mt 5:38–41

Don't have unrighteous anger
Mt 5:22

CROSS-REFERENCES

Luke 10:30–37

Romans 12:9–21

Philippians 2:1–11

CHAPTER 27

I n a dog-eat-dog world, there's unanimous consensus on how to respond to cold and cruel people—you give them a dose of their own medicine. Tit for tat? No indeed. More like *hit* for tat! Do unto others *after* (and even better, before) they do unto you.

Given that the world typically operates by the principles of retaliation and revenge, are we really surprised that so many conflicts—between siblings and spouses, neighbors and nations—linger for years, even decades?

The Bible offers a better way.

Kindness to enemies disrupts evil. When we've been wronged, the thought of "going off on someone" can feel very powerful. But all that does is make the environment more toxic and "give the devil a foothold" in our lives (Ephesians 4:27). Solomon said that, ironically, a gentle response has the real power to defuse someone's wrath (Proverbs 15:1). A thousand years later, Paul urged, "Do not be overcome by evil, but overcome evil with good" (Romans 12:21). It's the good (i.e., godly) response—the one that seems weak and wimpy—that has the most power to change the status quo.

Kindness to enemies breaks down walls. Think of unkind actions (and harsh reactions) as stones of mistrust and animosity. Over time, these callous cruelties combine to form thick walls that effectively separate individuals and groups from one another. Kindness, however, functions like a wrecking ball. Even the smallest act effectively removes a stone or two from the wall—and begins to pave the way for possible reconciliation.

Kindness to enemies models the gospel. The Bible says that before Christ's forgiveness, we were God's enemies (Romans 5:10). (And the Bible makes clear that this relational friction was our fault, not his.) God had every reason to "go off on us," but instead of treating us as our sins deserved, he showed us kindness. He came near in Jesus and did everything necessary to reestablish peace with us. Thus, when we forgive others the way he forgave us, we imitate the love and grace of God.

Reconciliation—not retaliation—is the way of the gospel.

Life Application

Hopefully you don't have any true "enemies," but probably you do have people in your life with whom you're not on the best terms. Maybe just the mention of their names makes you frown. Do this: Begin to pray regularly for those people. Pray also for God's direction on how you could model the gospel in the way you relate to them.

HOW TO RESPOND TO ENEMIES

Dealing with Enemies

Help them when they're in need
Ex 23:4–5

Don't rejoice in their downfall
Pr 24:17

Pray for them
Mt 5:44

Love them
Mt 5:44

Feed them when they're hungry (be kind to them)
2Ki 6:22–23; Ro 12:20

FRIENDS, NEIGHBORS & ENEMIES

CROSS-REFERENCES

Proverbs 25:21–22

Luke 6:27–36

John 15:18–25

PART 5

WORK, MONEY, AND BUSINESS

CHAPTER 28

What is a *steward*? In biblical times, those with great wealth and large estates would often appoint one qualified servant to be "over the house" (Genesis 43:19; 44:4). This "steward" would act as a kind of guardian, superintendent, and/or manager (Luke 16:2–3). As the chief administrator of all household affairs, the steward functioned like an ancient COO (chief operating officer) and CFO (chief financial officer).

What are the qualities of a steward? It was paramount that any person entrusted with such great responsibility would be characterized as the following:

- **Trustworthy.** Because he would have access to large sums of money and valuable property, integrity and faithfulness were essential (Matthew 25:14–30; Luke 16:10–13; 1 Corinthians 4:1–2).
- **Gifted.** Because of the complexity/difficulty of the task, certain skills and abilities were vital (1 Corinthians 12:28).
- **Wise.** Because the position called for frequent decision making, the steward needed to be insightful and discerning (Matthew 25:14–30).
- **Servant-minded.** Because a steward had one simple mission—to carry out the wishes of the master—he functioned less as a "boss" and more as a servant to the other servants within the household. The steward's job was to use all the resources allocated to him by the master to resource the other servants so that they could do their jobs effectively and efficiently (Colossians 3:23).
- **Compassionate.** Because stewards are caretakers and caregivers they must be concerned with distributing gifts and resources for the good of all (Genesis 2:4–9, 15; Matthew 14:13–21; Matthew 25:31–46; 1 Corinthians 12:12–28; James 2:14–17).
- **Content.** Regardless of how much they are entrusted with, all they have belongs to God, and they must look to him for all strength and wisdom (Philippians 4:11–13; 1 Timothy 6:6–10).
- **Loyal.** Because the steward must serve faithfully, remembering who they are and whose they are at all times (Matthew 6:19–21, 24; Luke 14:25–33).
- **Responsible.** Because caring for the master's possessions and wisely managing resources never ends (Genesis 41:37–45; Numbers 18:25–32; 2 Samuel 24:18–25; Matthew 28:16–20).

What does stewardship have to do with us? The biblical writers borrow this

WHAT HAS GOD ENTRUSTED YOU WITH?

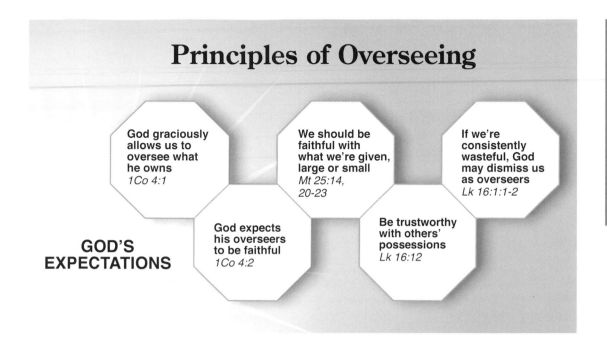

Principles of Overseeing

WORK, MONEY & BUSINESS

God graciously allows us to oversee what he owns
1Co 4:1

We should be faithful with what we're given, large or small
Mt 25:14, 20-23

If we're consistently wasteful, God may dismiss us as overseers
Lk 16:1-2

GOD'S EXPECTATIONS

God expects his overseers to be faithful
1Co 4:2

Be trustworthy with others' possessions
Lk 16:12

stewardship imagery and terminology to speak of how Christians should function in the church—not only monetarily, but with our whole lives. According to the Bible, in Christ we are all trusted servants/stewards in the great household of God (1 Corinthians 4:1; Ephesians 2:19). God assigns us the task of using whatever gifts we've been given to dispense grace (1 Peter 4:10) and to help other believers (Ephesians 3:2; Titus 1:7).

Why Stewardship Matters

The Bible makes clear that every believer faces a kind of eternal "job review" (2 Corinthians 5:10). What's more, Jesus told several parables that suggest that faithfulness for Christ in this life will give us greater opportunities for service in the world to come (Luke 19:12–27).

CROSS-REFERENCES

Psalm 24:1

Luke 19:11–27

1 Timothy 6:20

CHAPTER 29

The Bible talks extensively about money and makes this big, overarching point: *how we handle material wealth is a reliable indicator of our spiritual health.*

In brief, here's what the Bible says about money:

Money is a *blessing*. Scripture clearly teaches that all wealth comes from the Lord. God is gracious and generous to shower good things on his creatures. Many of the great saints of the Bible—Abraham (Genesis 13:2), Job (Job 1:2–3), and Solomon (1 Kings 10:14–29), for example—possessed enormous riches. But the blessing of money is surely not the only way God blesses his people (Philippians 4:11–13). In fact, the Bible says in so many words, "Pity the poor individual whose wealth is solely financial."

Money is a *trust*. The Bible is clear that God is the owner of everything (Psalm 24:1). We are only temporary stewards or short-term managers of the assets God places in our care.

Money is a *test*. Jesus put it this way: "Where your treasure is, there your heart will be also" (Luke 12:34). In other words, humans naturally wrap their hearts around whatever they value most. Thus, money reliably shows what a person loves, values, and trusts in.

Money is a *danger*. Money has a way of making us feel invincible (Psalm 52:7). The smug, self-satisfied soul can begin to think, *Why do I need to trust God when I have a financial portfolio that is growing by leaps and bounds?*

This is why God warns those he's blessed with worldly wealth against pride and forgetfulness (Deuteronomy 8:17–18). This is also why Jesus talked about how difficult it is for those with great wealth to enter the kingdom of heaven (Mark 10:23). Is money a blessing? Absolutely. Is money also a burden and a danger? Yes (1 Timothy 6:9–10).

Money is a *tool*. Jesus commanded us to be generous (Acts 20:35) and challenged us to "store up . . . treasures in heaven" (Matthew 6:20). Someone has wittily paraphrased his words this way: "You can't take it with you—but you can send it on ahead."

> *He is no fool who gives what he cannot keep to gain that which he cannot lose.*
>
> Jim Elliot, missionary-martyr

STEWARDS OF GOD'S MONEY

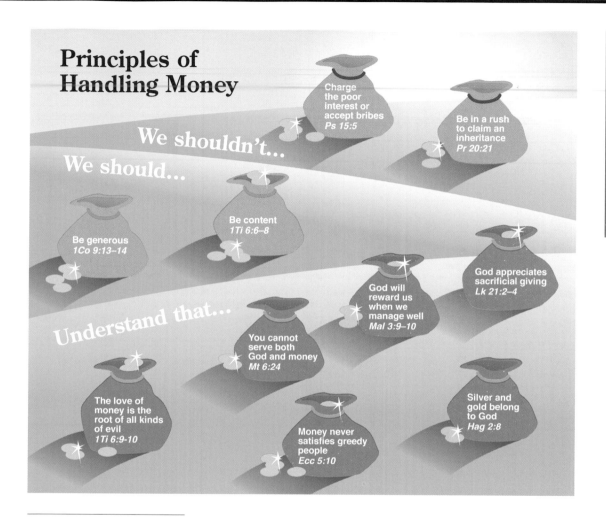

Principles of Handling Money

We shouldn't...

Charge the poor interest or accept bribes
Ps 15:5

Be in a rush to claim an inheritance
Pr 20:21

We should...

Be generous
1Co 9:13–14

Be content
1Ti 6:6–8

God appreciates sacrificial giving
Lk 21:2–4

God will reward us when we manage well
Mal 3:9–10

Understand that...

You cannot serve both God and money
Mt 6:24

The love of money is the root of all kinds of evil
1Ti 6:9-10

Money never satisfies greedy people
Ecc 5:10

Silver and gold belong to God
Hag 2:8

WORK, MONEY & BUSINESS

CROSS-REFERENCES

Exodus 36:5

Deuteronomy 10:14

Luke 12:33

CHAPTER 30

No doubt you've heard the complaint, "Why do certain preachers and churches talk nonstop about giving?" (Perhaps you've even said this yourself.)

While it's true that some overemphasize the subject, it's also true that the Bible talks frequently about money and giving. Jesus, in fact, talked more about these matters than he did about heaven and hell.

Here are three primary reasons giving is good:

Giving imitates God. It is God's very nature to give (Matthew 7:11). He is the giver of life (Nehemiah 9:6). He is the giver of food (Psalm 136:25). He gives wisdom (Proverbs 2:6), strength (Psalm 29:11), relief (Isaiah 14:3), and victory (Psalm 20:6). In truth, every good gift is from God (James 1:17). And of course God's greatest gift of all is his Son (John 3:16). In Jesus, God not only gave us all we would ever need but gave us the deepest desire of our hearts. When we give, we resemble our heavenly Father.

Giving expresses faith. It's easy to *talk* about faith in a theoretical, abstract way. However, in giving to the work of God, we put our money where our mouths are. Giving is a tangible display of the beliefs we profess. Unless one is convinced of the truth of the Bible (i.e., that all "my stuff" actually belongs to God, that people are lost without Christ, that this world is not all there is, and that "we must all appear before the judgment seat of Christ" [2 Corinthians 5:10]), why give one's hard-earned money to support the work of God's kingdom? One of the best-loved stories of the Gospels is Jesus marveling over the faith and generosity of a poor widow at the Jerusalem temple (Luke 21:1–4).

Giving erodes greed. It has been suggested that if we have a possession about which we think, *It would* kill *me to lose that*, perhaps we need to give that thing away before it kills us. Giving loosens the grip that money and things sometimes have on our hearts. As a spiritual discipline, giving combats the ever-present temptation of materialism (Luke 12:15).

> *A person needs to experience three conversions: the conversion of the head, the conversion of the heart, and the conversion of the pocketbook.*
>
> traditionally ascribed to Martin Luther

REASONS TO GIVE

Reasons to Give

Giving supports the Lord's work
Mal 3:10a

Giving is commanded.
Mal 3:8–9

Giving shows love *Jn 3:16*

Giving prompts thanksgiving.
2Co 9:11

Giving helps the poor
Ac 10:4

Giving results in blessing
Mal 3:10b; Ac 20:35; 2Co 9:6–8s

Giving is a privilege—a demonstration of grace.
2Co 8:3–6

CROSS-REFERENCES

Deuteronomy 16:17

2 Chronicles 31:5

Proverbs 28:27

Malachi 3:8

CHAPTER 31

WORK, MONEY & BUSINESS

The Bible makes clear that an individual who succumbs to the desire for more money and "stuff" puts himself or herself on a path to trouble. Look at all the dire things greed leads to:

- **Illegal/sinful acts.** Because of greed, Laban cheated his son-in-law, Jacob (Genesis 31:41); Achan stole forbidden loot from the conquered city of Ai (Joshua 7:21); Saul coveted and kept some spoils of war that God told him not to keep (1 Samuel 15:9); Ahab stole a vineyard from Naboth; and Judas betrayed Jesus (Matthew 26:15).

- **Endless discontent.** Proverbs 30:15 observes, "The leech has two daughters. 'Give! Give!' they cry." We see this insatiable hunger for more in the words of John D. Rockefeller, once the world's richest man. When asked how much money would be enough to satisfy him, he allegedly replied, "Just a little bit more."

- **Nagging worry.** Ecclesiastes 5:10 says, "Whoever loves money never has enough; whoever loves wealth is never satisfied with their income." We've all seen this verse lived out—people who scramble feverishly to protect themselves against any and every potential financial setback. While there's nothing wrong with hard work and saving for the future, at some point we have to trust the God who loves and cares for us. We have to rest in him and his promise to meet all our needs (Philippians 4:19).

- **Personal misery.** James warned those who were obsessed with hoarding riches, "Your gold and silver are corroded. Their corrosion will testify against you and eat your flesh like fire" (James 5:3).

- **Family woes.** Solomon warned, "The greedy bring ruin to their households" (Proverbs 15:27). Sure enough, we see evidence of this almost weekly in the news—from petty thefts to elaborate financial scams. Crime not only doesn't pay; it brings much grief to innocent loved ones and bystanders.

- **Apostasy.** The worst consequence of unchecked greed? Loving and trusting money eventually replaces loving and trusting God. Money becomes an idol, a substitute for God. Jesus put it plainly: "No one can serve two masters. Either you will hate the one and love the other, or you will be devoted to the one and despise the other. You cannot serve both God and money" (Matthew 6:24).

LOVING MONEY

Characteristics of Those Who Love Money

ACTION	RESULT
They fall into temptation *1 Ti 6:9*	**They are never satisfied** *Ecc 5:10*
They give in to foolish and harmful desires *1 Ti 6:9*	**They are cursed** *Mal 3:9*
They wander from the faith *1 Ti 6:10*	**They experience much grief** *1 Ti 6:10*

If your desires be endless, your cares and fears will be so, too.

Thomas Fuller, seventeenth-century pastor and writer

CROSS-REFERENCES

Psalm 49:10

Ecclesiastes 2:26

1 Timothy 6:7

CHAPTER 32

An idol is a "God substitute." Often it's a *good* thing (even a blessing from God) that we turn into an *ultimate* thing.

People can make an idol out of almost anything—food, sex, physical appearance, social status (prominence, popularity, platform), a job, a talent, a hobby, a relationship, a dream, or something else. Surely one of the most common and insidious idols is *worldly wealth.*

Why does money make a lousy "god"? Because unlike the one true God, riches are not any of the following:

- **Unchanging.** The stock market goes up and down. Interest rates rise and fall. A person's life savings can disappear in a single day. God, on the other hand, is always the same (Psalm 102:25–27). He's reliable, constant, sure, and certain. And because he never changes, his love, grace, mercy, and kindness don't fluctuate either (Hebrews 13:8). They're tied to his faithful character, not to any other factors.
- **Eternal.** Think of this: whatever size financial portfolio you manage to accumulate in this life, it becomes utterly useless to you the moment you draw your final breath (Luke 12:20). You can surely pass on your assets, but you can't take them with you (Ecclesiastes 5:15). Worldly wealth is aptly named. It's for this world only; then it becomes irrelevant to the owner—*unless* the owner has exchanged some of his or her worldly currency for heavenly treasure (Matthew 6:19–20).
- **All-powerful.** A multibillionaire is diagnosed with stage-four pancreatic cancer. With his or her immense financial resources, he can pursue every conceivable treatment option on earth. A blessing? Absolutely! However, there's no guarantee that the wealthy person's great economic advantages will lead to a cure and to health. Wealth isn't omnipotent; only God is.
- **Able to satisfy.** You've heard the old saying "Money can buy a lot of things, but it can't buy happiness." It's true. Wealth can't alleviate guilt. It can't solve the problems of loneliness, bitterness, insecurity, and fear. It can alter our lifestyles but is powerless to transform our hearts in deep ways. Only Jesus can do such things (John 10:10).

Trusting in wealth is futile. As God said through the prophet Isaiah, "Turn to me and be saved, all you ends of the earth; for I am God, and there is no other" (Isaiah 45:22).

IS WEALTH EVIL?

WORK, MONEY & BUSINESS

Principles of Wealth

GOD'S PART

God provides the ability to produce wealth
Dt 8:18; Ecc 5:19

PRINCIPLES TO REMEMBER

Wealth can be short-lived
Pr 23:5

Wealth can cause you to turn away from God
1Ti 6:9–10

OUR PART

Remember God when he gives you wealth
Dt 6:10–12

Don't gain wealth dishonestly
Ps 62:10

Honor God with your wealth
Pr 3:9–10

Treasure heavenly things, not earthly things
Mt 6:19–21

Don't trust in wealth
1Ti 6:17

Be generous with your resources
1Ti 6:18–19

CROSS-REFERENCES

1 Chronicles 29:12

Proverbs 23:5

Malachi 3:6

Mark 4:19

CHAPTER 33

WORK, MONEY & BUSINESS

For many, work is something to be endured. For others, it's something to joke about (probably so they won't cry). The Bible takes a different view:

Work is *holy*. The Bible begins with a glorious account of the creation of the world. At the end of six days of "work" (see Genesis 2:2–3)—that is, creating, making, separating, gathering, organizing, naming, and so on—the triune God is described as making humans in "his own image" (one clear implication in this phrase is that they'll be workers too, just as he is). Sure enough, the Lord commissions his human masterpieces to "subdue" the earth (Genesis 1:28). He puts them in a garden to "work it and take care of it" (Genesis 2:15). It's important to note that all of this happens *before* sin—with all its unpleasant effects—enters the world.

Work is *hard*. When Adam and Eve rebel against God by eating the forbidden fruit in Eden (Genesis 3:6), the consequences aren't only *spiritual* (i.e., separation from God), *personal* (i.e., guilt, fear, and shame; see Genesis 3:10), and *relational* (i.e., friction with one other). Another result is *occupational*. God tells Adam that his working of the earth will become "painful toil" (Genesis 3:17). For the first time in the Bible, "sweat" is mentioned (v. 19). Thus, all the frustrations of your job—uncooperative coworkers, demanding clients, computer woes, and the like—are actually traceable to this long-ago event.

Work can bring *happiness*. *Work* and *happiness* in the same sentence? In Ephesians 6, Paul urges servants to serve their employers as though they are serving Christ himself (vv. 5–8). When we do this, our labors become labors of love. We're not just "making a buck" or "trying to pay bills," we are also using our brains and/or brawn, our gifts and abilities to both honor God and bless others. As *that* becomes our mission and motive, we are able to find great fulfillment and gladness in even menial tasks.

With a biblical perspective, no one can say, for example, "I'm *just* a highway worker." You're a highway worker who builds the roads that enable the truck driver to deliver bread to the sandwich shop so that an hourly worker can make sandwiches for a dad who is trying desperately to connect with his wayward son.

Do you see the difference? As one wise saint said, "All work done for Christ has a glory."

WORK AS GOD'S GIFT

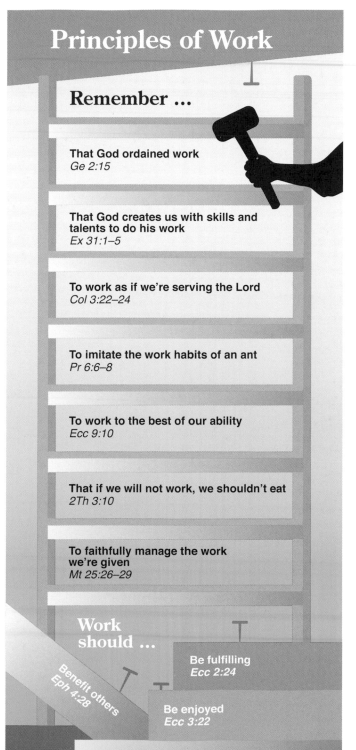

Principles of Work

Remember ...

That God ordained work
Ge 2:15

That God creates us with skills and talents to do his work
Ex 31:1–5

To work as if we're serving the Lord
Col 3:22–24

To imitate the work habits of an ant
Pr 6:6–8

To work to the best of our ability
Ecc 9:10

That if we will not work, we shouldn't eat
2Th 3:10

To faithfully manage the work we're given
Mt 25:26–29

Work should ...

Benefit others
Eph 4:28

Be fulfilling
Ecc 2:24

Be enjoyed
Ecc 3:22

CROSS-REFERENCES

2 Chronicles 34:11–12

Proverbs 10:4; 12:11

CHAPTER 34

Whether you are the CEO of a multimillion-dollar corporation, a small-business owner, the manager of a division/department, or the supervisor of a shift, the Bible has clear instructions for how you are to treat those who work for (or under) you.

At minimum, every boss needs to keep in mind what the Bible says about the following:

A supervisor's motive. Ultimately, every employer should be motivated by the same goal that the Bible gives for his or her employees: "working for the Lord" (Colossians 3:23). The glory of God—not merely profits or one's brand or market share—should be what drives a business owner's decisions and activities. An employer should constantly ask, "How can I run this business and/or treat my employees in a way that makes God smile?"

A supervisor's mindset. The sobering warning of the apostle Paul to masters (i.e., employers, bosses, overseers, etc.) is, "You . . . have a Master in heaven" (Colossians 4:1). In other words, don't forget that even though we may have multiple workers under us who are accountable to us for what they do on the job, we are under *God* and accountable to *him* for how we run our workplace and treat our workers.

A supervisor's manner. The Mosaic law told Israelite farmers not to go back and harvest overlooked sheaves of grain or unpicked olives. "Leave what remains" was the divine command so that there might be something for the less fortunate, and "so that the LORD your God may bless you in all the work of your hands" (Deuteronomy 24:19–22). Here was the principle of generosity, of using one's business or livelihood in benevolent and altruistic ways. Business donations to nonprofits would be one modern version of this practice.

Some Habits of Good Employers

Model the work ethic you want your employees to have. Catch your employees doing good things and praise them. Smile. Offer timely job reviews and fair raises. Do what's right (not just what's required by law). Don't treat your workers the way that harsh boss treated you back in the day.

CROSS-REFERENCES
Deuteronomy 24:15
Matthew 24:45
James 5:4

What the Bible Says About (and To) Bosses

Good bosses...

- ☑ **Pay their workers** *Jer 22:13*
- ☑ **Pay their workers *fairly*** *1Ti 5:17–18*
- ☐ **Pay their workers *promptly*** *Lev 19:13*
- ☐ **Don't take advantage of their workers** *Dt 24:14*
- ☐ **Don't show favoritism in the workplace** *Col 4:1*
- ☐ **Aren't harsh with their workers** *Eph 6:9*
- ☐ **Value excellent employees** *Lk 7:2*
- ☐ **Promote faithful employees** *Pr 27:18*
- ☐ **Rectify legitimate worker grievances** *Job 31:13-14*
- ☐ **Remember that God rescues his people from cruel bosses** *Ex 3:7–9*

CHAPTER 35

In our ever-changing economy, more and more people are moonlighting, starting small businesses, or opting to create LLCs and use their skills as self-employed workers. These kinds of work/business arrangements offer some distinct advantages over traditional employment, but they can be stressful too. For those brave souls who are "occupationally adventurous," the Bible gives lots of practical advice:

Maintain priorities. In one of his parables (Luke 14:16–19), Jesus portrayed (unflatteringly) those who let their business interests come before all else. Don't confuse making a living with making a life.

Plan carefully. Jesus told another parable about a successful businessman who became obsessed with planning far into the future (Luke 12:16–21). James, the half brother of Jesus, warned against this same danger and urged a submissive, "whatever" spirit toward the perfect purposes of God (James 4:13–17). We should hold all our plans with an open hand.

Find balance. Psalm 39:6 speaks of those who go "around like a mere phantom; in vain they rush about, heaping up wealth without knowing whose it will finally be" (Psalm 39:6). While the Bible does praise diligence and encourage hard work (Proverbs 10:4; 13:4), it also stresses resting in the Lord (Psalm 127:1–3), trusting that he will take care of all the issues that are beyond our control.

Pursue excellence. This is a surefire way to be successful in business (Proverbs 22:29), provided we also have integrity in dealing with customers, suppliers, and clients. We will be known as either honest or dishonest (Leviticus 19:35–36).

Through it all, it can be helpful to remind ourselves that God created work. It was his gift to Adam and Eve in the Garden of Eden. It offered humanity purpose, dignity, and a chance to worship through the fulfilling of God's command to subdue creation.

When sin entered the world, work was corrupted and fell under a curse. Adam and Eve's pristine Garden of Eden grew thorns, which made their daily tasks difficult and—at times—even dreadful.

When we approach work, it is understandably easy to look at the task ahead of us and focus on the thorns. Every job has them. The challenge for those who want to follow Jesus is to look past the thorns and find pleasure in the gift of work God has given. It's from him and serves as a place we can grow and glorify him.

WISDOM ABOUT WORK AND BUSINESS

Guidelines About Work and Business

WORK HARD

Hard work is fulfilling, but laziness leads to dissatisfaction
Pr 13:4

Generous, fair people will be blessed
Ps 112:5

REMEMBER THAT...

Laziness leads to poverty; hard work results in wealth
Pr 10:4-5

Work like an ant that has no supervisor but works diligently
Pr 6:6-8

God hates dishonesty in business
Pr 11:1

Having wealth can be stressful
Ecc 5:12

Proverbs 13:11 is a great principle for business owners. It speaks of gathering money little by little and making it grow. In other words, avoid business deals that seem too good to be true. Beware of greed. Instead, be patient and realistic in your business projections, planning, and execution.

CROSS-REFERENCES

Proverbs 11:1; 12:11

Ecclesiastes 5:12

CHAPTER 36

WORK, MONEY & BUSINESS

We hear much talk today about the "separation of church and state." Some who advocate for this idea are simply trying to avoid the pitfalls of government-sponsored religion. Others are hoping, however, to squelch any and every expression of faith from the public square. This latter view argues that one's faith should be a wholly private matter that does not in any way affect public policy.

Given this wide spectrum of viewpoints, how are people of faith—especially those who work in jobs under the auspices of a secular government—supposed to live out their faith?

Fortunately, the Bible features a number of characters who worked in a variety of "government jobs." By and large these individuals seemed to embrace a "show-and-tell" policy. Remember when you had show-and-tell time in elementary school and students took turns both *displaying* and *describing* some item? Well, in the Bible, people of faith in positions of power and influence are typically seen exhibiting their faith through their *character/conduct* and their *conversation*. In other words, there's a *visual* element—showing what they believe with their lives—and a *verbal* element—telling what they believe with their lips.

Here are two great questions for all workers (and especially those working in government):

- **Am I a person of integrity—like Daniel (see Daniel 6)?** Or put another way, if my colleagues decided to do a secret, comprehensive examination of my life—interviewing people and examining my emails, texts, and internet usage, for example—what would they find? Evidence that I am a follower of Jesus? Or proof that I am a hypocrite?
- **Am I willing to speak truth to power—like Daniel (see Daniel 5)?** In other words, when I see corruption or injustice, do I clam up or speak up?

Pray for those who are close to "power." Pray that they will have the character and courage to shine the light of Christ in dark places.

CROSS-REFERENCES

Matthew 2:1–11
Acts 4:1–20; 5:27–29

SERVING IN GOVERNMENT

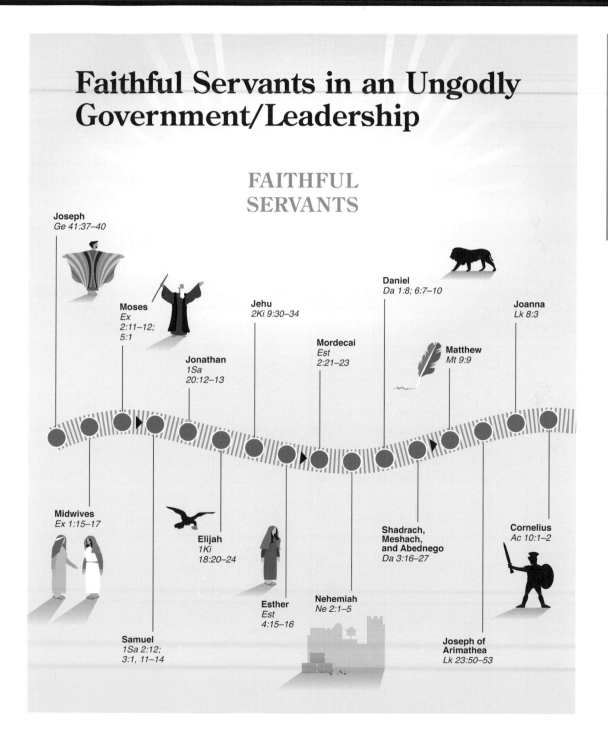

Faithful Servants in an Ungodly Government/Leadership

FAITHFUL SERVANTS

Joseph
Ge 41:37–40

Moses
Ex 2:11–12; 5:1

Jonathan
1Sa 20:12–13

Jehu
2Ki 9:30–34

Mordecai
Est 2:21–23

Daniel
Da 1:8; 6:7–10

Matthew
Mt 9:9

Joanna
Lk 8:3

Midwives
Ex 1:15–17

Elijah
1Ki 18:20–24

Esther
Est 4:15–16

Nehemiah
Ne 2:1–5

Shadrach, Meshach, and Abednego
Da 3:16–27

Cornelius
Ac 10:1–2

Samuel
1Sa 2:12; 3:1, 11–14

Joseph of Arimathea
Lk 23:50–53

PART 6

STRUGGLES AND SUFFERING

CHAPTER 37

STRUGGLES & SUFFERING

Hollywood has conditioned us to like feel-good stories with happy endings. Sadly, real life doesn't often work this way. The Bible shows some saints suffering and experiencing relief. It shows others suffering until their last breath. Take Job, for example. He got his health back (although he did of course eventually die; see 42:17). And his lost wealth was restored (42:12). And he even had ten more children and multiple grandchildren in his old age (42:13–16). However, we can be sure he mourned the loss of his ten oldest children all the remaining days of his life.

Here are four biblical truths about suffering:

1. Suffering involves painful waiting. As slaves in Egypt, the Israelites had to wait decades, if not centuries, for deliverance (Exodus 2:23). Abraham and Sarah waited a quarter century for God to make good on his promise of a son (Genesis 12:2–4; 21:1–5). Joseph spent two years languishing in prison for a crime he didn't commit (Genesis 41:1). In the New Testament, the bleeding woman of Mark 5 lived with her condition for twelve years. Sometimes there are exceptions—Jesus turned Lazarus's funeral into a party after just four days (John 11:1–37). This is not normative, however.

2. Suffering reveals God. Although most saints taste divine deliverance in this life and most of us get morning shouts of joy

after nights of weeping (Psalm 30:5), others endure endless "jeers and flogging . . . [chains] and . . . prison" (Hebrews 11:36). In some cases, God doesn't powerfully deliver *out of* suffering. Rather, he empowers his suffering saints to endure—and even shine—*in the midst of* lifelong pain.

3. Suffering can produce good. God used Joseph's mistreatment to save his entire family (Genesis 37–50). Moses spent forty years in brokenness and obscurity (Exodus 2) so that he might acquire the humility needed to lead the Israelites out of Egyptian bondage. Out of the grim death of his Son, Jesus, God offered eternal life to the world (John 3:16). When we trust God and submit to his plan, he can redeem and use for good even the worst things in our lives.

4. Suffering *will* eventually cease. The Bible assures us that one day death, mourning, crying, and pain will pass away (Revelation 21:4). In the words of author J. R. R. Tolkien, everything sad is going to come untrue. God will restore, remake, and renew the world to its original—that is, perfect—"factory settings." The book of Revelation reveals the ultimate happy ending.

CROSS-REFERENCES

Job 23:10

1 Peter 4:12

Revelation 2:3

PEOPLE WHO SUFFERED AND GOD'S RESOLUTION

People Who Suffered and God's Resolution

SUFFERING		RESOLUTION
Loss of family and property *Job 1:14-19; 2:7-8*	**JOB**	**Restoration of family and property** *Job 42:10,12,13,16,17*
Sold into slavery *Ge 37:26-28;* *39:20a*	**JOSEPH**	**Raised to power** *Ge 41:39-40* *Ge 39:20b-23*
Slaves in Egypt *Ex 1:8-14*	**THE ISRAELITES**	**Depart Egypt with treasures** *Ex 12:31-36,* *40-42*
A lonely widow *Ru 1:3-5*	**NAOMI**	**A new family** *Ru 4:13-17*
Childless *1Sa 1:6-11*	**HANNAH**	**A son is born** *1Sa 1:19-20*
David on the run *1Sa 19:11–12*	**DAVID**	**David becomes king** *2Sa 2:1–7*
Years of suffering *Mk 5:25–28*	**WOMAN** **WITH THE ISSUE** **OF BLOOD**	**Healed in a moment** *Mk 5:29* *Mk 5:32–34*
Death of a brother *Jn 11:17–22*	**MARY** **AND MARTHA**	**Brother raised to life** *Jn 11:41–44*
The world is broken by sin *Ge 3:1–19*		**The world is restored by God** *Rev 21:1–8*

HUMANITY AND THE WORLD

CHAPTER 38

We've seen it countless times in cartoons—a tiny devil perches on a character's shoulder and whispers tantalizing suggestions. Typically this is followed by the immediate appearance of an angel on the other shoulder, urging the character to do the right thing.

This cartoonish picture of temptation is oversimplified, but we can all attest to the reality of an inward tug-of-war between right and wrong. Thankfully the Bible gives some powerful reminders to believers in Christ when they feel a pull toward sin:

In Christ you're a new person. Second Corinthians 5:17 says that believers are a "new creation." In temptation, therefore, we don't appeal to "the better angels of our nature"; we remember that we have a new nature. "The old has gone, the new is here!" Paul exclaimed. We're no longer the same people we used to be. Given that fact, why would we keep living the way we used to live? Galatians 5:17 speaks of this internal struggle between a Christian's flesh (i.e., the unredeemed human nature we inherited from Adam) and our new nature (see 2 Peter 1:4), which is energized by God's Spirit who indwells believers. The point of course is that while our old nature does still long for sinful things, our new, true nature longs to please God. Those new, holy desires *are* there—whether we feel them or not. They explain why, whenever we choose to do right, we always feel good inside.

In Christ you have new power. Consider how Paul prayed for the Ephesian Christians: "I pray . . . that you may know . . . his incomparably great power for us who believe" (Ephesians 1:18–19). Later he prayed, "I pray that out of his glorious riches he may strengthen you with power through his Spirit in your inner being" (Ephesians 3:16). God's power is greater than the pull of any temptation (1 Corinthians 10:13).

In Christ you have a perfect example. Christ's temptation in the desert is the supreme example of successfully overcoming temptation. Every time Satan tried to focus Jesus' attention on worldly concerns, Jesus turned his attention back toward God and his Word (Matthew 4).

Life Application

Spiritual maturity is that process of ignoring the loud, fleshly passions that scream for fulfillment on the surface of our lives and listening instead to the new, holy desires that God has planted in our hearts. It's asking ourselves, *What do I really want in this situation—the temporary pleasure of sin or the eternal joy of obedience?*

FACING TEMPTATION

Dealing with Temptation

Don't be led into temptation
Mt 6:13
Lk 11:4

Pray that you won't give in to temptation
Mt 26:41
Mk 14:38
Lk 22:40
Lk 22:46

God doesn't tempt us – the devil does
Mt 4:1
Mt 4:3
Mk 1:13
Lk 4:2
Jas 1:13

Jesus understands how it feels to be tempted
Heb 2:18
Heb 4:15

Use the Word of God to defeat Satan
Mt 4:4, 7, 10;
Lk 4:4, 8, 12

We are tempted by our own evil desires
Jas 1:14

Wanting wealth leads to temptation and destruction
1Ti 6:9

When helping a troubled friend, be careful to not be tempted
Gal 6:1

We overcome the world through faith in God
1Jn 5:4

We overcome evil with good
Ro 12:21

God helps us when we're tempted
1Co 10:13

CROSS-REFERENCES

Ezekiel 36:26–27

Romans 8:5

Galatians 5:16

CHAPTER 39

STRUGGLES & SUFFERING

Kinds of Suffering

In one sense, all people experience suffering. How could it be otherwise? We are fallen people living in a fallen world. Religious or not, devoted to Christ or not, everyone faces natural disasters, disease, and—eventually—death. This kind of suffering is nondiscriminatory. It is universal.

In another sense, people of faith suffer solely because of their religious beliefs. Jesus predicted this, soberly warning his followers, "If they persecuted me, they will persecute you also" (John 15:20). Except during certain eras and in specific places where government has been sympathetic to the Christian faith, followers of Jesus have experienced persecution since the time of Jesus. (And of course the Jewish people have been persecuted since the time of Moses.)

Degrees of Suffering

Religious persecution can (and often does) take a variety of forms. It can be personal (severed friendships), familial (being disowned by parents and/or siblings—Jesus spoke of this in Luke 21:16), emotional and verbal (threats, insults, and bullying; see 2 Chronicles 32:10–15 and Psalm 42:10), social (being excluded/ostracized from groups), occupational/financial (loss of a job, boycotts of one's business), civil (official government oppression; see Acts 5:41), and physical (beatings, torture, even execution; see Acts 12:2).

Truths about Suffering

Suffering is inevitable. Although it's not a promise that most Christians like to memorize and post on social media, Paul told Timothy, "Everyone who wants to live a godly life in Christ Jesus will be persecuted" (2 Timothy 3:12).

Suffering is transformative. God is able to use our suffering to shape us into the image of Christ (Romans 8:28–29). Here's how Peter explained it: "And the God of all grace . . . after you have suffered a little while, will himself restore you and make you strong, firm and steadfast" (1 Peter 5:10). James said, "Consider it pure joy, my brothers and sisters, whenever you face trials of many kinds, because you know that the testing of your faith produces perseverance. Let perseverance finish its work so that you may be mature and complete, not lacking anything" (James 1:2–4).

Suffering is temporary. Although we share in the sufferings of Christ, we are promised that we will one day share in his glory (Romans 8:17).

ENDURING SUFFERING

Facing Pain
1 Peter

Remember ...

To not be surprised when you suffer
4:12

That you're blessed when you're insulted for Christ
4:14

To not suffer for doing wrong
4:15

Responses

Rejoice when you suffer for Christ
4:13

Continue to be faithful and do good
4:19

Don't be ashamed for suffering as a Christian
4:16

The apostle Paul made this stunning announcement about suffering: "For our light and momentary troubles are achieving for us an eternal glory that far outweighs them all" (2 Corinthians 4:17). How does this perspective give strength and hope in the face of trouble?

CROSS-REFERENCES

Acts 9:16

Hebrews 11:25

1 Peter 2:20

CHAPTER 40

Even if we aren't going through a difficult life struggle right now, chances are someone we love is. What can we do to help those who hurt?

Remember the Golden Rule. Jesus said, "So in everything, do to others what you would have them do to you, for this sums up the Law and the Prophets" (Matthew 7:12).

Bite your tongue. Remember Job's counselors? History doesn't look favorably upon them, but in actuality, for the first week of Job's terrible trial, they were exemplary friends (Job 2:11–13). They sat in silence with their devastated buddy. They didn't pontificate, lecture, or attempt to "speak for God" by offering explanations for Job's troubles. They simply gave the gift of their presence. Their silence shouted, "We can see you're hurting, old buddy. We don't understand this, and we can't fix your situation, but we're with you. We're here. We love you." It was when Job began venting and processing out loud—both necessary parts of the grief process—that his friends started theologizing and suggesting that Job must have done something wrong to deserve his plight.

Ask yourself, "Do I find insensitive comments to be comforting? Do I like people preaching at me when I'm suffering?" Of course not. So don't be guilty of such things when you attempt to sympathize with someone who's hurting.

Open your eyes and ears. Paul tells us to look out for the interests of others (Philippians 2:4). Ask yourself, "What tangible act can I do that would be helpful here?" Then be observant. Pay attention to comments. Notice the little things you could do that would be big blessings—running errands, bringing meals, offering child care, doing housework, providing lawn care, and so on.

When it is time to speak, speak truth. Eventually the one who is suffering will be ready to talk about the pain they are experiencing. When that time comes, listen, and respond with the truth of the Bible. Job's hope was this: "I know that my redeemer lives, and that in the end he will stand on the earth" (Job 19:25). The love of our Redeemer is what you encourage with and share. No one is abandoned. God is always with us, and he is well acquainted with grief, and every other form of suffering we endure. He is with us now to lead us into the freedom that can only be found by trusting completely in him and resting in the peace he wants to share with all people.

Be patient. Job's wife ran out of patience and told him to "curse God and die." She did not see any point in allowing the

TOUGH TIMES

suffering to continue. Suffering will last varying lengths of time for different people, and as true friends, bearing the truth of Christ and the freedom of the Spirit in their lives, we must stick with them, no matter how long it takes. Remember the patience God has with all of us. Remember the pain he has endured so that we may share in his life. You are in others' lives to share that amazing patience and enduring love with them.

Grief isn't a short-term proposition. People don't "get over" devastating losses in a few weeks or months. This is why the ancients referred to the quality of patience as being "longsuffering." Be patient toward those who hurt.

CROSS-REFERENCES

Isaiah 51:3

John 14:1

1 Thessalonians 5:11

Encouragement for Those Suffering

God is compassionate toward suffering people
2Co 1:3

Jesus understands your suffering and can help you
Heb 2:18; 4:15–16

For believers, all things work together for good
Ro 8:28

God's power emerges in your weaknesses
2Co 12:9

God strengthens you in your suffering
Isa 41:10

God will take care of you
Mt 6:31–34

You don't have to be anxious; God will give you peace
Php 4:6–7

God will restore you after suffering
1Pe 5:10

CHAPTER 41

STRUGGLES & SUFFERING

Every time we turn around, there is more bad news—a terrible tragedy here, a weather catastrophe there. When our days are full of mixed signals from world leaders, the stock market, bosses, and struggling children, it's easy to become anxious and full of dread. For some, thoughts like these are related to deep anxieties or reactions that require special care or professional help.

For most, however, our anxious thoughts reveal our own drive to be in control or our refusal to depend on God. In situations like this, the Bible says a lot about battling fretfulness and fear.

There's a reason that one of the most common commands in the Bible is "Do not be afraid / do not fear." God knows we are prone to freaking out, and he wants to show us a better way.

Dumping the bad habit of worry. The Jewish prophet Isaiah (who lived among people with ample reasons to fret) wrote a song of praise to God in which he said, "You will keep in perfect peace those whose minds are steadfast, because they trust in you" (Isaiah 26:3). Peace of mind comes when our minds are steadfast—that is, when we fix our thoughts on God and place our trust in God.

How can we develop such a God-focused mindset? Worry is simply a bad habit we picked up along the way. For many it's second nature—automatic like breathing. The good news, however, is that if we learned this bad habit, we can unlearn it.

Learning the new habit of trust. Successful athletes know that the way to overcome their fear and doubt is to replace those thoughts and feelings with ones of confidence and courage. Our battle with worry is similar. Instead of continuing to meditate on hypothetical "what if," worst-case scenarios (which is all worry is), we learn to meditate on—and regard as true—the promises of God. We replace fear with faith, and we rest in God's perfect character, his good heart, and his faithful love (and we remember that he is in charge of outcomes).

Becoming (and remaining) care-less. The apostle Peter, who knew a thing or two about stress, once urged an ancient group of beleaguered Christians, "Cast all your anxiety on him because he cares for you" (1 Peter 5:7). The word "cast" means to hurl, to throw with great force. In other words, the moment you feel worry starting to creep in and weigh you down, heave those cares onto God.

Life Application

Consider memorizing Psalm 139:23–24 and making it your daily prayer to God.

HOW TO DEAL WITH ANXIETY

Battling Fear

The number of verses in Psalms that portray the writers' raw human fear versus their decision to trust in God no matter the situation

Trust
50

Those who know your name trust in you, for you, LORD, have never forsaken those who seek you. *9:10*

In God I trust and am not afraid. What can man do to me? *56:11*

I will say of the LORD, "He is my refuge and my fortress, my God, in whom I trust." *91:2*

Fear
35

My thoughts trouble me and I am distraught. *55:2*

I am overwhelmed with troubles and my life draws near to death. *88:3*

Search me, God, and know my heart; test me and know my anxious thoughts. *139:23*

CROSS-REFERENCES

Psalm 118:6

Matthew 6:25–33

Philippians 4:6–7

CHAPTER 42

STRUGGLES & SUFFERING

Worry can be unhealthy. Moderate anxiety can spark headaches, muscle tension, and short-term memory loss. Even more chilling? Medical research has demonstrated a link between chronic worry and serious disorders of the immune and digestive systems—as well as coronary artery disease. Anxiety itself comes in a variety of forms. A person wakes up feeling vaguely *antsy*. This subconscious *unease* gives way to conscious *concern*, which then morphs into overt *fretting*. Unchecked, this persistent *worry* turns into paralyzing *fear*, even *panic*. When you think about it, worry is nothing more than forgetting the reality of God and then meditating on worst-case scenarios.

Here are three reasons Christians should seek to unlearn the habit of being anxious and develop the holy habit of trusting in the Lord:

1. **Worry is *unrealistic*.** Worry dismisses the greatest reality of all—almighty God. It creates a fictitious world in which a good, gracious, loving, merciful, wise, promise-keeping God is no longer present and active. Such a scenario will never be true.

2. **Worry is *un-Christian*.** Christianity is distinct in that it claims the following: God, because of his great love and grace, came to live among us in Jesus Christ (John 1:1, 14). Jesus' mission was to seek and save us (Luke 19:10) and to give us life to the full (John 10:10). Even when we were sinners, Jesus died for us (Romans 5:8). Jesus rose from the dead, meaning he's alive forevermore (and has vowed to be with his followers always; Matthew 28:20). If God has done all this for us, then no matter our circumstances, we can be assured of his constant love, care, and provision (Romans 8:31–32).

3. **Worry is *unhelpful*.** Jesus said it himself—worry adds nothing to our lives (Matthew 6:25–34). Stewing over an unpaid bill doesn't pay the bill. Agonizing over your company's impending layoffs won't secure your job. Worry doesn't change anything—at least not for the better.

> *Worry does not empty tomorrow of its sorrow. It empties today of its strength.*
>
> Corrie ten Boom

CROSS-REFERENCES

Luke 10:41; 21:34

Philippians 4:6–7

WHY WORRY IS A WASTE

Overcoming

God understands your anxiety
Ps 139:23

God will sustain you
Ps 3:4-6

God can turn difficulties around
Ps 18:28

God will protect you
Ps 3:1–3

God cares about you and your anxiety
1Pe 5:7

God will be with you
Jos 1:9

PART 7
THE SUPERNATURAL

CHAPTER 43

Bring up the subject of "spiritual warfare" and some people will look at you like you just stepped off the *Mayflower*. But this isn't some quaint, old-fashioned notion, nor is it a man-made idea.

The Bible outlines spiritual conflict. Ephesians 6:10–12 mentions "the devil's schemes," "our struggle," and "spiritual forces of evil." Elsewhere the apostle Paul urges Timothy to "fight the good fight of the faith" (1 Timothy 6:12) and to "join with me in suffering . . . like a good soldier of Christ Jesus" (2 Timothy 2:3). And the apostle Peter tells believers the devil is "your enemy" and warns them to be on high alert (1 Peter 5:8).

The Bible defines the enemy. The Bible identifies the primary enemy of God's people: Satan (Job 1:12; Acts 26:18). Among other names, he is also referred to as "the devil" (Luke 4:13; 1 John 3:8), "the god of this age" (2 Corinthians 4:4), "the father of lies" (John 8:44), and "the evil one" (Matthew 13:19). Jesus described him as having legions of demons (i.e., fallen angels) who are loyal to him (Matthew 12:24–26; cf. Revelation 12:9).

The Bible offers a defense. Scripture tells Christians that God has given them both defensive armor and offensive weaponry for this fight. Paul reminds believers that we can ward off the devil's accusations (Revelation 12:10) and temptations (Matthew 4:3) by putting on the belt of truth (or integrity), the breastplate of righteousness, the footwear of peace, and the helmet of salvation, and taking up the shield of faith and the sword of the Spirit, which is the word of God (Ephesians 6:13–17).

The Bible reveals the outcome. The Bible tells us that Jesus has won. The writer of Hebrews said that Jesus came so that "by his death he might destroy him who holds the power of death—that is, the devil" (Hebrews 2:14). The apostle John wrote, "The reason the Son of God appeared was to destroy the devil's work" (1 John 3:8).

By his death and resurrection, Jesus forgave sin, abolished death, and defeated the great enemy of our souls. Even though Satan and his demons futilely fight on, their power has been broken. No wonder John went on to declare triumphantly to his Christian readers, "The one who is in you is greater than the one who is in the world" (1 John 4:4).

FIGHTING EVIL

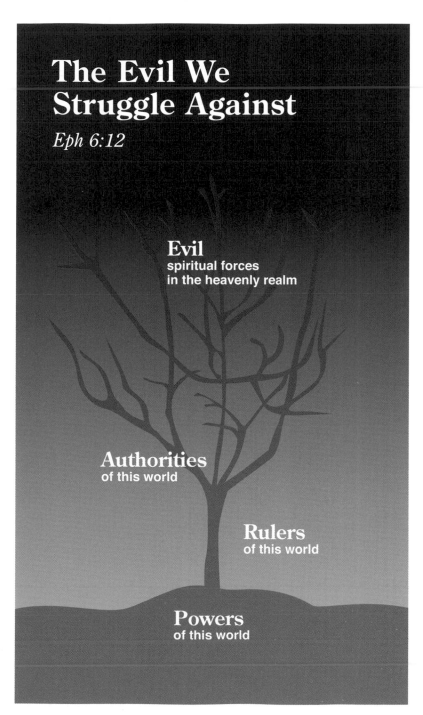

The Evil We Struggle Against

Eph 6:12

Evil
spiritual forces
in the heavenly realm

Authorities
of this world

Rulers
of this world

Powers
of this world

CROSS-REFERENCES

Luke 9:42

Ephesians 4:26–27

James 2:19

CHAPTER 44

When it comes to the devil and demons, author C. S. Lewis noted that most people tend either to dismiss the subject as mere superstition or to become obsessed with the idea. Both perspectives, he suggested, are dangerous. Here is what we can say for sure:

Satan is *real*. Jesus spoke matter-of-factly (and often) about the reality of Satan and demons (Luke 10:18; 11:18, 24–28; John 8:44). Thus, to deny their existence is to discount the teaching of Jesus, to conclude that the Son of God was either ill-informed or lying.

Satan is *vicious*. Jesus called the devil "a murderer" (John 8:44). John called him "the accuser of our brothers and sisters" (Revelation 12:10)—and in our souls, following moments of failure, we have all heard his hateful, withering accusations. The apostle Peter likened the devil to a "roaring lion," prowling about "looking for someone to devour" (1 Peter 5:8). No wonder he warned, "Be alert and of sober mind."

Satan is *sneaky*. The apostle Paul talked about "the devil's schemes" (Ephesians 6:11). The Greek word translated "schemes" is the word from which we get our English word *methods*. It means "procedures" or "machinations" and has overtones of being crafty, cunning, wily, and deceptive. In other words, Satan is the consummate fast-talking salesman who is forever trying to "pull a fast one" on unsuspecting people. We can't lower our guard.

Satan is *defeated*. The first man, Adam, succumbed to Satan's beguiling temptation (Genesis 3:1–8), but Jesus, the Son of Man and "the last Adam" (1 Corinthians 15:45), never did (Matthew 4:1–11; Hebrews 4:15; 1 Peter 2:22). Israel failed to trust God and sinned in the wilderness (Numbers 14), but Jesus did not (Luke 4:1–13; 1 John 3:5). By his sinless life and sacrificial death, Jesus paid the price for sin. What's more, in his incarnation, death, and resurrection, Jesus was able "to destroy the devil's work" (1 John 3:8). While Satan attempts to inflict some final damage in the earth's waning hours, his end is already sealed (Revelation 20:10).

Christians can glory in this truth—that the Lord of the universe who lives inside them (Colossians 1:27) is greater than (1 John 4:4) the sinister serpent (Revelation 20:2), who is only the temporary "god of this age" (2 Corinthians 4:4). The day is coming when God will crush Satan under our feet (Romans 16:20).

SATAN: REAL AND ACTIVE

Satan's Attributes

Characteristics

He's proud
Eze 28:17

His wisdom is corrupted
Eze 28:17

He's our enemy
1Ch 21:1

He's evil
Eph 6:16

Actions

He accuses
Zec 3:1

He tempts
1Th 3:5

He ignores rules & laws
2Th 2:8

He opposes God's plans and ways
Mt 16:23

He slanders
Rev 13:5–6

CROSS-REFERENCES

John 13:2; 14:30

1 John 3:10

CHAPTER 45

As grim and unpopular as the subject may be, the Bible speaks plainly about a real place called hell. According to a plain reading of Scripture, hell is where unrepentant, unbelieving people will spend eternity.

The Names of Hell

The Old Testament uses the Hebrew word *Sheol* to describe the destination of all the dead (both righteous and unrighteous). *Sheol* means "the pit" or "the grave." Not until New Testament times do we find clear distinctions being made between the final destinies of believers and unbelievers.

The New Testament writers use the Greek words *Hades* (comparable to the Hebrew *Sheol*) and *Gehenna* to speak of hell. *Gehenna* refers to the Valley of Hinnom, an actual ravine outside the southern wall of Jerusalem. This site was notorious for two reasons: (1) ancient pagan practices (including child sacrifice; see 2 Kings 23:10) took place here, and (2) the valley became, over time, an open landfill where refuse and the bodies of executed criminals were thrown and incinerated. As a result, fires burned there almost continuously.

The Nature of Hell

The descriptions of hell in the Bible are both terrible and terrifying. Hell is said to be a place

- where unforgiven unbelievers are "shut out from the presence of the Lord and from the glory of his might" (2 Thessalonians 1:9)
- of "chains of darkness" (2 Peter 2:4)
- of "blackest darkness" (Jude 13)
- of "everlasting contempt" (Daniel 12:2)
- of "eternal punishment" (Matthew 25:46)
- of "torment" (Luke 16:23) and "agony" (16:24)
- "where there will be weeping and gnashing of teeth" (Matthew 8:12; 22:13)

The Bible also uses abundant fire imagery in its descriptions of hell. The Gospel of Matthew, for example, quotes Jesus as speaking of "the fire of hell" (literally "Gehenna"; see 5:22), "the blazing furnace" (13:42), and "the eternal fire prepared for the devil and his angels" (25:41). Mark speaks of hell as being a place "where the fire never goes out" (9:43, 48). John, in the book of Revelation, sees a "lake of fire" (20:15), a "fiery lake of burning sulfur" (21:8).

Christians have had heated debates over how to interpret these phrases. Are they meant to be taken literally or figuratively? By using the flames, smoke, and stench of Gehenna to refer to hell, Jesus provided

WHAT HELL IS LIKE

a graphic picture of how awful eternity will be for those who reject the grace of God. However one interprets these fiery references, we can safely conclude that just as heaven will be infinitely more wonderful than we can possibly imagine, so hell will be far worse than anyone can fathom.

CROSS-REFERENCES

Daniel 12:2

Matthew 10:28

John 3:36; 5:28–29

What the Bible Says About Hell

There will be eternal separation from God
Rev 20:15

There will be continual punishment
Mt 25:46

There will be unending sorrow and anger
Mt 13:42

There will be insatiable thirst
Lk 16:24

There will be unquenchable fire
Mk 9:43

There will be unappeasable pain and suffering
Rev 14:10–11

God's wrath will be unleashed
Rev 14:10

The Bottom Line on Hell

1. God doesn't want *anybody* going there. The Old Testament depicts God pleading with the wicked to turn from their evil ways (Ezekiel 33:11). The New Testament states that God "wants all people to be saved and to come to a knowledge of the truth" (1 Timothy 2:4). He is "not wanting anyone to perish, but everyone to come to repentance" (2 Peter 3:9).

2. God has made a way for *everybody* to avoid hell. In sending Jesus to pay for our sins and be judged in our place (1 John 4:10), God has shown his great love (John 3:16) for us. Our debt has been paid. Our pardon has been purchased.

CHAPTER 46

THE SUPERNATURAL

In the Bible, the word *heaven* or *heavens* sometimes refers simply to the sky, earth's atmosphere, or outer space (Psalm 8:3). Mostly, however, *heaven* is used to mean the place where God is enthroned, where he lives with his angels (Psalms 11:4; 14:2; Jonah 1:9; Matthew 5:16), and where the righteous go after this life is over (2 Kings 2:11; Philippians 3:20).

Synonyms for the Life to Come

Jesus called heaven "my Father's house" (John 14:2) and "paradise" (Luke 23:43). In a story about heaven (Luke 16:22), he used banquet terminology to speak of a deceased beggar as being at "Abraham's side." (Abraham was viewed as the consummate father of faithfulness and righteousness.)

The Bible also speaks often of "eternal life" (John 5:24). Jesus defined such life this way: "Now this is eternal life: that they know you, the only true God, and Jesus Christ, whom you have sent" (John 17:3). Thus, eternal life is, in its essence, relationship with God, and heaven is enjoying the presence and fellowship of God. In a real sense, Christians get a *taste* of heaven here on earth when they trust in Christ (John 3:16), and they experience it *fully* after they depart this world.

The Nature of the Life to Come

- **It's actual and real.** The night before his crucifixion, Jesus spoke matter-of-factly about going away to "prepare a place" for his followers (John 14:1–5). He also promised, "I will come back and take you to be with me that you also may be where I am" (v. 3).
- **It's a place of reward.** The Bible makes clear that faithfulness to Christ here will lead to rewards there (2 Corinthians 5:10; 2 Timothy 4:8; James 1:12). Serving the Lord in the present will lead to opportunities for greater service to God in the future (Luke 19:11–27; Revelation 22:3).
- **It will undergo a "total makeover" in the last days of earth.** Astonishingly, the Bible indicates that the existing heaven will be shaken (Haggai 2:6) and will pass away (Mark 13:31). However, God will create "new heavens and a new earth" (Isaiah 65:17; 66:22; 2 Peter 3:13; Revelation 21:1).
- **This new heaven and new earth will be free of all the painful and destructive effects of sin** (Revelation 21:1–4). In resurrected, glorified bodies (Philippians 3:20–21) the redeemed will live joyfully and eternally in God's presence. We will get to live the life that Adam and Eve forfeited.

A GLIMPSE OF HEAVEN

What Heaven Is Like

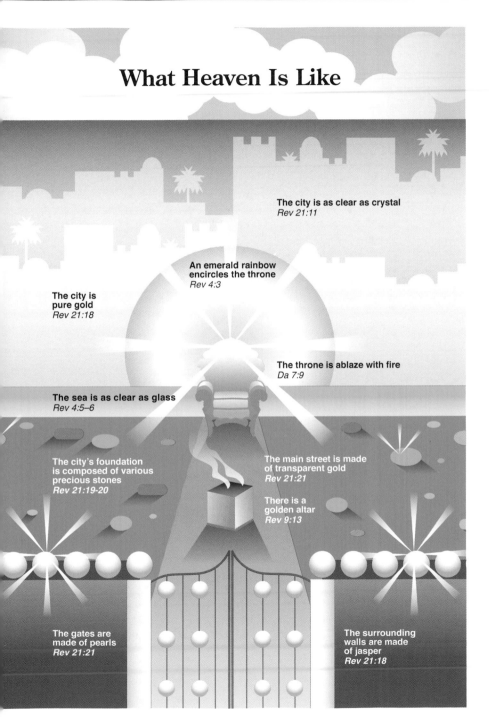

The city is as clear as crystal
Rev 21:11

An emerald rainbow encircles the throne
Rev 4:3

The city is pure gold
Rev 21:18

The throne is ablaze with fire
Da 7:9

The sea is as clear as glass
Rev 4:5–6

The city's foundation is composed of various precious stones
Rev 21:19-20

The main street is made of transparent gold
Rev 21:21

There is a golden altar
Rev 9:13

The gates are made of pearls
Rev 21:21

The surrounding walls are made of jasper
Rev 21:18

CROSS-REFERENCES

Deuteronomy 26:15

Luke 10:20

Acts 7:56

PART 8

SIN AND THE SOLUTION

CHAPTER 47

If you think sin is a big subject in the Bible, you're right. The King James Version uses the word "sin" about 750 times—and that's not counting related words like "transgression," "iniquity," "guilt," and "evil."

What is the essential biblical teaching on this topic?

Sin is defiance of God. We minimize sin when we reduce it to a list of petty misbehaviors—lying, cheating, stealing, and so on. Sin is a posture of the heart (Jeremiah 17:9). It's an inward, rebellious stance that resents God, rejects and rebuffs him, and continually replaces him with lesser things. Sin refuses to trust God and says instead, "I don't have to honor you, acknowledge you, or obey you. I can live however I please" (see Romans 1:18–25).

Sin is a universal problem. The father of the human race essentially infected all his offspring (Romans 5:12). This prompted someone to note, "We're not only sinners because we sin—we sin because we're sinners." No one is immune. We're all guilty (Romans 6:23) because sin permeates human nature.

Sin is tricky and powerful and enslaving. The Bible speaks of an evil being—the devil or Satan—who tempts people to doubt or ignore what God has said and encourages us to follow our sinful urges (Ephesians 2:2; 1 Thessalonians 3:5). Sin is such a powerful force that it even uses God's perfect and holy law to incite sinful desires within us (Romans 7:5–12). According to Jesus, giving in to sin doesn't make us free—it makes us slaves (John 8:34).

Sin meets its match in Jesus. The Bible says that Jesus "appeared once for all at the culmination of the ages to *do away with sin* by the sacrifice of himself" (Hebrews 9:26, emphasis added).

Life Application

The promise of the gospel of Christ is that Jesus forgives sin (Colossians 1:14). What amazing grace! What's more, by uniting believers to himself (Romans 6:9–14), Jesus saw to it that we would be "set free from sin" (Romans 6:18). As we trust in this truth—and the one who lives inside us—we find that we no longer have to give in to sin. Its power and hold over us are gone. However, when we do stumble and fall, we have an advocate with the Father—Jesus Christ, the Righteous One (1 John 2:1).

WHAT THE BIBLE SAYS ABOUT SIN

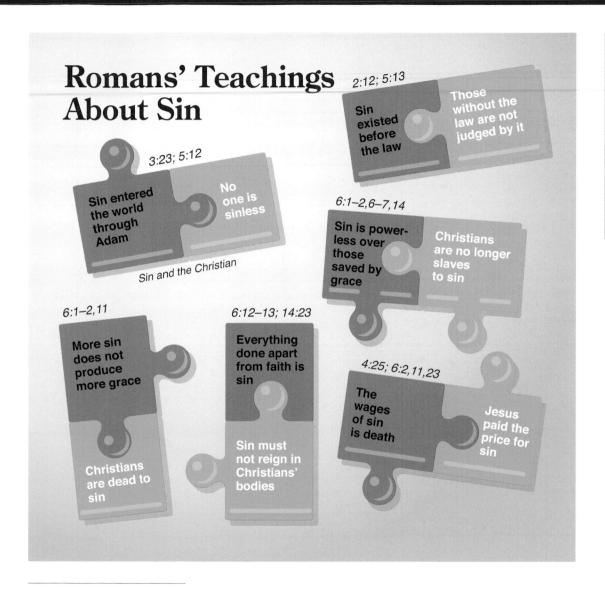

Romans' Teachings About Sin

2:12; 5:13
Sin existed before the law — Those without the law are not judged by it

3:23; 5:12
Sin entered the world through Adam — No one is sinless

Sin and the Christian

6:1–2,6–7,14
Sin is powerless over those saved by grace — Christians are no longer slaves to sin

6:1–2,11
More sin does not produce more grace — Christians are dead to sin

6:12–13; 14:23
Everything done apart from faith is sin — Sin must not reign in Christians' bodies

4:25; 6:2,11,23
The wages of sin is death — Jesus paid the price for sin

CROSS-REFERENCES

Micah 7:18–19

Romans 5:8

1 Corinthians 15:3–4

2 Corinthians 5:21

CHAPTER 48

Religion typically works like so:

1. Rules are laid down ("Here's how to please God").
2. Consequences are spelled out ("Violate these rules and suffer accordingly").

Jewish history says that Moses received a set of rules (the Torah) from God at Mount Sinai (scholars count 613 separate commands). The remainder of the Jewish Bible (i.e., the Christian Old Testament) records Israel's long, futile struggle to live according to these standards.

Enter Paul, a young Jew fiercely devoted to God's law (Acts 9). Initially a violent opponent of the "Christian movement," Paul became its biggest proponent when he unexpectedly encountered the resurrected Jesus. He spent the rest of his life spreading the message that sinful people are made right with God, not by keeping rules, but by trusting in Jesus.

In the letter we know as Romans, Paul argued that God gave his law to reveal (a) his holiness and (b) our sinfulness. In other words, the law served primarily to underscore humanity's need—not for rules but for a Rescuer, a Savior. Some of Paul's key points:

Living by law is ugly. Although the law itself is "holy, righteous and good" (Romans 7:12), it has a way of bringing out the worst in us. Law keepers get obsessed with the question "How am I doing?" and thus become self-absorbed. Depending on their performance, they vacillate between pride and despair.

Living by law is futile. Paul emphatically said, "No one will be declared righteous in God's sight by the works of the law" (Romans 3:20). Trying to solve our sin problem with rules is like trying to treat cancer with MRIs and CT scans. The law can't cure us—it can only diagnose our problem.

Living by law is unnecessary. Romans 8:1–4 says God sent Jesus to do (a) what we could never do (i.e., keep the law) and (b) what the law could never do (i.e., set us free). In Christ we are forgiven and transformed. The rest of Romans shows how, with the help of the indwelling Spirit, we live for God—not to earn salvation, but to show our gratitude for the salvation he has provided in Christ.

WHAT THE BIBLE SAYS ABOUT THE LAW

Romans' Teachings about the Law
Romans 2:12—10:4

What the Law Can Do	*What the Law Cannot Do*
Judge those who follow it *2:12–13*	**Declare people righteous who follow it** *3:20*
Reveal sin to people *3:20; 4:15; 7:8*	**Set people free from sin** *8:3*
Increase trespass *5:20*	**Provide grace** *6:14*
Culminate in Christ *10:4*	**Justify people** *3:28*

SIN & THE SOLUTION

Life Application

Ask yourself these questions:

1. Do I think, consciously or subconsciously, that God likes me better when I "keep his rules"?
2. Is my hope in "what I do for God" or in "what God has done for me in Christ"?

CROSS-REFERENCES

Galatians 3:1–15

Philippians 3:1–14

Hebrews 10:1–25

CHAPTER 49

Is it a sin to be tempted? Many people are surprised to find out that temptation—although it may be difficult or undesirable—is not in itself sinful. We know this because Jesus was tempted "in every way," yet he remained sinless (Hebrews 4:15). Temptation is simply the enticement to do evil. There's no sin as long as we, like Jesus, refuse such offers (Luke 4:1–13).

While temptation is not a sin in itself, it should not be taken lightly. The Bible offers key principles for dealing with the allure of sin.

When tempted we can't become passive. The Old Testament shows Joseph running away (literally) from the married woman who was trying to seduce him (Genesis 39:12). In the New Testament, the apostle Paul encourages his young protégé Timothy to "flee all this" (i.e., envy, strife, abusive language, the love of money, etc.; 1 Timothy 6:11).

In another place, Paul reminds believers that although we all face temptation, God will never let us face more temptation than we can stand. He will always "provide a way out so that you can endure it" (1 Corinthians 10:13). This means that when temptation comes, we can't mull it over. We have to be active, even violent, in our decisiveness. We have to look for—and urgently take—God's "way out," as Jesus so carefully did when he was tempted in the desert.

If we play with temptation's fires, we will get burned. When Cain was furious that God had rejected his offering—but had accepted his brother Abel's sacrifice—he received this gracious warning from God: "Sin is crouching at your door; it desires to have you, but you must rule over it" (Genesis 4:7). Sadly, instead of fighting his anger, Cain surrendered to his violent impulses—and became the world's first murderer.

The sad story of David and Bathsheba (2 Samuel 11) is another example of this simple, sober truth. When David spied the beautiful Bathsheba bathing on a nearby rooftop, he should have shut the blinds, turned away, called a friend, engaged in some productive royal endeavor—something, anything. Instead, he opened his heart to temptation's alluring voice. His fate was sealed the moment he inquired about her (v. 3). In short order, he "sent messengers to get her . . . and he slept with her" (v. 4).

Sin always has consequences. The enemy, seizing upon our fleshly weaknesses, whispers, "No one will ever know." Of course this is a diabolical lie. *We* will know, and more importantly, *God* will know. And others may eventually find out too!

SIN'S STRATEGY

The Process of Sin
James

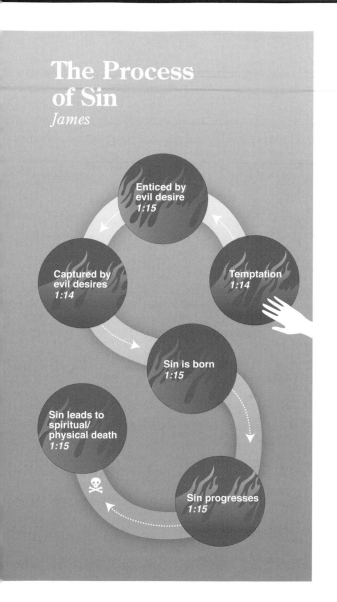

- Enticed by evil desire
1:15
- Captured by evil desires
1:14
- Temptation
1:14
- Sin is born
1:15
- Sin leads to spiritual/physical death
1:15
- Sin progresses
1:15

But even if our sin never becomes a big, public scandal, it will at least become a source of private pain. David spoke of the internal anguish resulting from his sin: "When I kept silent, my bones wasted away through my groaning all day long" (Psalm 32:3).

Real Hope for Sinners

The good news of the Bible is that "if anybody does sin, we have an advocate with the Father, Jesus Christ, the Righteous One" (1 John 2:1). Jesus is both our substitute and our advocate (i.e., our defense attorney). No wonder John reminded believers, "If we confess our sins, he is faithful and just and will forgive us our sins and purify us from all unrighteousness" (1 John 1:9).

CROSS-REFERENCES
Romans 7:11
1 Corinthians 15:34
Hebrews 3:13

CHAPTER 50

At first glance the "acts of the flesh" in Galatians 5:19–21 seem to be a kind of expanded New Testament update of the Ten Commandments (i.e., Fifteen Sins to Avoid). But this passage is more than a spiritual list of don'ts:

Sin is deep and complicated. If we look closely at this "sin list" (and others like it, e.g., Romans 1:26–31; 1 Corinthians 6:9–10), it's clear that sin involves more than wrong behaviors. Notice the mix of wrong actions *and* attitudes. Experience shows us this too—our outer conduct is *always* prompted by inner convictions. In short, we pursue whatever things our hearts tell us will bring us life and happiness. This is why Jesus insisted in Luke 6:45 that sin is, first and foremost, a heart issue. Unless and until a person's heart is touched and transformed by Christ, all the lists and laws in the world, whether religious or civil, are powerless to keep us from sin.

Sin is wide-ranging. Notice that the sins cited here range from private "impurity" to public "riotous behavior," and from easy-to-hide "envy" to out-in-the-open "rage." In other words, sin runs the gamut. It's varied. Like cancer it can take different forms and wreak havoc anywhere.

Sin is sometimes subtle, sometimes overt. Some sins cause scandals, others elicit yawns. Perhaps you've noticed the human tendency to "rank" sins. For example, *Being envious of my friend's new home might be wrong, but using a racial slur is much worse, and abusing a child is unthinkably evil.* Interestingly, the Bible suggests that God doesn't think like this. He doesn't "rank" sins. Because he is holy (i.e., perfect and sinless), a person who commits even one sin is just as guilty as the person who breaks every law in the book (James 2:10).

Sin is devastating. Paul's list is meant to serve as a cautionary tale. Think about the real-life consequences of succumbing to any one of these sins. A life marked by immorality or rage or envy or drunkenness—where does such a life lead? Is that the kind of life you want? Notice the dire warning at the end of Galatians 5:21: "Those who live like this will not inherit the kingdom of God."

> In contrast to the undesirable "acts of the flesh" (Galatians 5:19), pray that God will produce in you the "fruit of the Spirit" (vv. 22–23).

THE SINFUL NATURE

Works of the Sinful Nature
Galatians

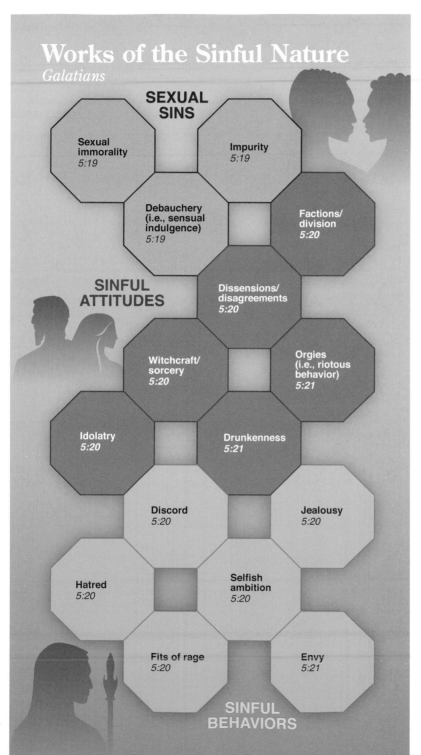

SEXUAL SINS

Sexual immorality
5:19

Impurity
5:19

Debauchery (i.e., sensual indulgence)
5:19

Factions/ division
5:20

SINFUL ATTITUDES

Dissensions/ disagreements
5:20

Witchcraft/ sorcery
5:20

Orgies (i.e., riotous behavior)
5:21

Idolatry
5:20

Drunkenness
5:21

Discord
5:20

Jealousy
5:20

Hatred
5:20

Selfish ambition
5:20

Fits of rage
5:20

Envy
5:21

SINFUL BEHAVIORS

CROSS-REFERENCES

Ephesians 4:25–31

Colossians 3:5–7

2 Timothy 3:1–7

CHAPTER 51

We speak so frequently of "sin," we often forget all it signifies. However, it's only when we remember the terrible meaning and consequences of sin that we are able to fully appreciate God's great salvation.

What Sin Is

The Bible uses a number of words to help us grasp the basic nature of sin. The Hebrew word *chata* means to "miss the mark" or "deviate." (The New Testament Greek equivalent is *hamartia*.) Another Hebrew word, *pasha*, conveys the idea of "rebellion"; *avah*, the idea of "deliberate distortion"; and *sagah*, the notion of "straying from the right way."

Put all this together and sin is ugly indeed. Sin is resenting God's rule and pridefully refusing to worship him as God. Sin is treason (an attempted coup against the King of the universe). Sin is betrayal (leaving the Lover of our souls and chasing after other, lesser gods).

And sin isn't just what we *do*—our long list of wrong speech and actions. Sin is *in* our spiritual DNA; it permeates our human nature. We're all infected because we inherited our rebellious tendencies from our original forefather, Adam (and "foremother," Eve).

What Sin Does

Sin ruins. When Adam and Eve essentially told God, "We will live however we please," they plunged the entire world into chaos and misery. Disease? Disasters? Death? Despair? None of these terrors existed in Paradise. They were released in the world only after sin reared its head. Addressing them might be complicated. Understanding where they originated is not.

Sin separates. One of the saddest verses in Scripture is Genesis 3:9. There God cries out to the cowering man and trembling woman who are hiding in the bushes of Eden, "Where are you?" Soon the two are hurling accusations, just before God removes them altogether from the garden.

Sin enslaves. The rest of the Bible tells the story of all God did to liberate people suffering under the effects of sin. Sinful people are at the mercy of their own sinful desires. What's worse, they live under oppressive systems and sinful leaders.

Only a deliverer from heaven could provide the necessary rescue.

Life Application

Take a few minutes today to prayerfully search your heart. Is there any unconfessed sin? If so, acknowledge it. Thank God for the forgiveness available in Christ. Praise him for his ample grace that is always more than enough to wash away your failures and wrong choices.

THE BARRIER FORMED BY SIN

How Does Sin Separate Us From God?

There is more to sin than failing to follow a set of laws or meet specific religious obligations. It is not only about what we do but also about who we are in relationship to God. Sin shatters humanity's connection with God in a way that cannot be repaired by paying fines or serving sentences.

Effects of Sin	What This Means For Us
FALLEN STATE OF THE WORLD God created a perfect world, but because of Adam and Eve's sin, the entire world suffers disasters, diseases, destruction, and death. *Ge 1:31; 3:17–18; Ro 8:20–22*	*The effects of sin are greater than what we see in our personal choices. We regularly hear about or ourselves experience earthquakes, hurricanes, and incurable diseases. But God gives us hope. And one day, the excruciating pain of this world will be replaced with indescribable joy.*
FALLEN STATE OF HUMANITY Every human is sinful because of Adam and Eve's disobedience. *Ge 3; Am 5:12; Ro 3:23; 14:11*	*Sin is more than breaking the Ten Commandments; it is any imperfect choice, thought, or action such as giving in to temptation, acting selfishly, or neglecting those in need. God wants us to live righteously every day and, with the help of the Holy Spirit, we can.*
BROKEN RELATIONSHIP BETWEEN GOD AND PEOPLE God is holy—sinless—and cannot have association with anything that is sinful. Judgment of sin is death and eternal separation from God. *Lev 11:45; 1Sa 2:2; Mt 25:31–46;*	*The effects of sin are deep and severe. Those who are too consumed with themselves to place their trust in Jesus and remain closed off to others' needs cannot become reconciled with God. Without the forgiveness of sin, which Jesus offers freely, no one will be permitted into God's presence in the afterlife.*
URGENT NEED FOR REPENTANCE AND SALVATION Salvation is available to everyone, but only those who follow Christ and trust him to forgive their sin can be reconciled to an eternal relationship with God. No one knows when their time on earth is up; the time for repentance and salvation is now. *Lk 15:11–32; Heb 8:12; 2Pe 3:9*	*God is patient and merciful; he wants all people to return to him in repentance. He understands, in his infinite wisdom, the imperfections of human nature. The love of Christ offers a chance for hope and salvation. Just as Christ was resurrected from the dead, so we too are resurrected from the spiritual death of sin.*

CROSS-REFERENCES

Psalm 32

Isaiah 53:5–6

Ephesians 1:7

CHAPTER 52

Many people assume *salvation* means "forgiveness of sins now and/or the guarantee of heaven when I die." Of course *salvation* does mean this, but it also means so much more.

The meaning of *salvation*. The biblical word translated "salvation" means, "save," "keep from harm," "rescue," "heal," or "liberate." It conveys the idea of being spared from destruction and death. For example, David says in Psalm 18:3, "I have been saved from my enemies" (he is speaking there of literal, human foes). Also, in the gospels, Peter (Matthew 14:30) and the other disciples (Matthew 8:25) cry out to be "saved" from drowning. These stories symbolize a problem that goes beyond mere physical danger and salvation that can be received from the risen King Jesus. Likewise, in the context of Jesus' crucifixion (Mark 15:30–31), "save" is used in the sense of "rescue from death," yet it carries overtones of a much greater meaning than simply deliverance from physical death (Matthew 27:49; John 12:27; Hebrews 5:7). Salvation can refer to physical or spiritual rescue.

The scope of salvation. Spiritual salvation is astonishing in its breadth. Scholars like to point out that salvation means that believers were *justified* (i.e., forgiven and declared righteous in God's sight—past tense—when they put their faith in Christ's gracious sacrifice for sin; Romans 5:1). What's more, salvation includes believers being *sanctified* (i.e., experiencing freedom from sin's power—present tense—because of God's indwelling Holy Spirit). Finally, salvation culminates in believers one day being *glorified* (i.e., removed—future tense—from the very presence of sin and made to be like Christ in heaven). No wonder some describe the breathtaking salvation that Christ provides like this: "We have been saved. We are being saved. We will be saved."

The riches of salvation. The biblical writers employ a number of terms and concepts in their attempts to describe salvation in all its power and beauty. *Regeneration* means that God grants new, eternal, spiritual life to those who previously were spiritually dead (Titus 3:5). *Conversion* means that God grants us the grace to turn from our sin to him (Acts 15:3; 26:18). *Imputation* means that God "charges" our sins to Christ and "credits" us with his perfect righteousness (Romans 5:12–19). *Redemption* means that God paid the price necessary to buy us out of our slavery to sin (Ephesians 1:7). *Reconciliation* means that God brings rebels like us back into right relationship with himself (Romans 5:10). *Adoption* means that God makes us his very own children and heirs (Romans 8:15).

THE GIFT OF SALVATION

What Is God's Plan for Salvation?

Adam and Eve's disobedience to God condemned the world to sin, brokenness, and death. Because of sin, humanity's relationship with God was severed. But in his love, God provided a way—the only way—to reconcile sinful people to himself. Jesus endured the punishment for humanity's sin by dying on the cross. Through his death and resurrection, he conquered the power of sin and death so that people could receive forgiveness for sin and have life with God for eternity. Salvation is a gift from God for all who choose to receive it and commit to following him. Faith in Christ—not belonging to a church or doing good works—is the only requirement for salvation.

CROSS-REFERENCES

John 3:1–7

Hebrews 12:14

1 John 3:2

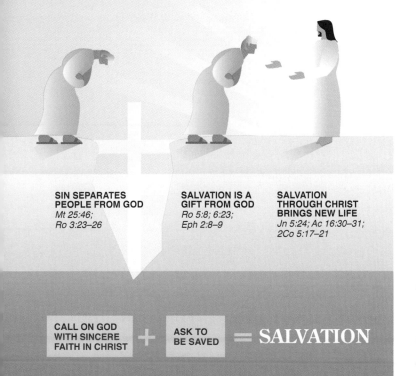

SIN SEPARATES PEOPLE FROM GOD
Mt 25:46;
Ro 3:23–26

SALVATION IS A GIFT FROM GOD
Ro 5:8; 6:23;
Eph 2:8–9

SALVATION THROUGH CHRIST BRINGS NEW LIFE
Jn 5:24; Ac 16:30–31;
2Co 5:17–21

CALL ON GOD WITH SINCERE FAITH IN CHRIST + ASK TO BE SAVED = SALVATION

Life Application

The writer of Hebrews warned believers not to "ignore so great a salvation" (2:3). You can obey this command by doing the following:

- Examination—continually studying all that God has done for you in Christ
- Exultation—praising and thanking God for his all-encompassing deliverance
- Evangelism—sharing the good news of salvation with someone else today

CHAPTER 53

We've all seen the person who dabbles in dieting and plays at exercise. We've also seen the person who is fiercely committed to eating right and hitting the gym. The difference is like night and day, isn't it? True commitment involves an "all in" mindset. Nowhere is this truer than in following Jesus.

Following Jesus is an either/or proposition. Again and again Jesus reminded people that following him was an either/or, not a both/and, commitment.

A person can't "sort of" follow Jesus any more than a woman can be "kind of pregnant." Either she is or she isn't. Either we follow Jesus or we don't. The choice is clear: in or out. "Whoever is not with me is against me," Jesus said (Luke 11:23). There's no fence straddling in the kingdom of God. No going back and forth. We have to choose decisively. We can have Jesus or the world—but we cannot have both.

Following Jesus is a messy process. We don't always get it right. In fact, sometimes we listen to our fleshly desires and wander away. Knowing what's right, we deliberately do the wrong thing. That's when a follower of Jesus must rely on other gospel dualities—that although we are unholy, he is holy; although we are sinful, he is gracious; although we deserve judgment, he gives us mercy (John 18:15–27; Romans 7:14–25).

Following Jesus results in a wonderful product. What did Jesus tell his first followers? "Follow me, and I will send you out to fish for people" (Mark 1:17). He was saying, If you follow me, I will make you into something you are not. I will transform you. What's more, I will use you in my own epic mission to seek and save those who are lost (Luke 19:10).

Following Jesus means we can be changed personally and also be instrumental in helping others find new life.

Life Application

Look at the Light and Darkness infographic. Consider carefully each either/or statement of Jesus. Ask the Lord to show you any situations, people, or things in your life that might be discouraging your wholehearted commitment to Christ. Pray about each one, asking the Lord for the grace and strength to be his faithful follower.

CROSS-REFERENCES

Deuteronomy 30:19

Joshua 24:15

1 Kings 18:21

Mark 9:40

THE COST OF FOLLOWING JESUS

Saints and Sinners

Jesus paints a stark contrast between those who follow him and those who don't

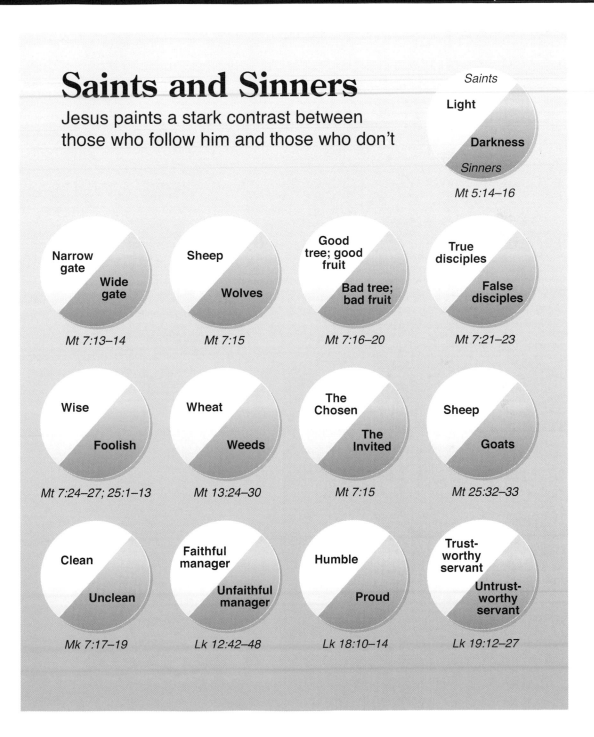

Saints
Light
Darkness
Sinners
Mt 5:14–16

Narrow gate / Wide gate
Mt 7:13–14

Sheep / Wolves
Mt 7:15

Good tree; good fruit / Bad tree; bad fruit
Mt 7:16–20

True disciples / False disciples
Mt 7:21–23

Wise / Foolish
Mt 7:24–27; 25:1–13

Wheat / Weeds
Mt 13:24–30

The Chosen / The Invited
Mt 7:15

Sheep / Goats
Mt 25:32–33

Clean / Unclean
Mk 7:17–19

Faithful manager / Unfaithful manager
Lk 12:42–48

Humble / Proud
Lk 18:10–14

Trustworthy servant / Untrustworthy servant
Lk 19:12–27

CHAPTER 54

The Bible *does* distinguish between two types of people—the godly and the ungodly. As the infographic to the right shows, we see this emphasis in the Psalms. However, throughout the Bible we see this dichotomy explained using a kaleidoscope of other terms and images—both woeful and wonderful. For example:

- The world is made up of *unbelievers*—those who don't/won't believe in Jesus (1 Timothy 5:8)—and *believers* (Acts 15:40).
- Unbelievers are *unrepentant* (Romans 2:5); believers are *repentant*—that is, they have turned from sin to God in humility and faith (Acts 3:19; 20:21).
- Unbelievers are spiritually *dead* (Ephesians 2:1–5), whereas those who trust Christ are made *alive* (Ephesians 2:5).
- Unbelievers are said to be under the just *condemnation* of a holy God because of their sin (Romans 1:18; 2:4; 5:18); believers, however, enjoy *justification* and *pardon* (Romans 5:18).
- Unbelievers are *in bondage* to sin (Romans 6:6, 16–18); believers have been *set free* from sin (John 8:36).
- Unbelievers *owe a great spiritual debt* to God because of sin (Colossians 2:14), while believers have been *ransomed and redeemed* (1 Corinthians 6:20; 7:23)—their debt is paid in full.
- Unbelievers are described as *lost*, and believers are described as *found* (Luke 15).
- The lost are *far away* from God; the found have been *brought near* in Christ (Ephesians 2:13).
- The lost are spiritually *blind* (2 Corinthians 4:4); those who have been found by Jesus, the Light of the World (John 9:5), are able to *see* (Luke 4:18–19).
- Unbelievers make themselves God's *enemies* (Romans 5:10)—a nightmarish thought. But believers are called the Lord's *friends* (John 15:14–15).

Life Application

Any one of these promises to believers would give reason to rejoice for an entire lifetime. Contemplating all of them together leaves a person speechless, even breathless.

Do this: Take some time to pray for the people in your life who do not yet know Jesus by faith. Ask the Father in heaven to draw them to his Son (John 6:44). Then pray for opportunities to "give the reason for the hope that you have" (1 Peter 3:15).

BELIEVERS VERSUS UNBELIEVERS

The Godly vs. the Ungodly

Psalms paints a clear picture of the ways of the godly and the ungodly

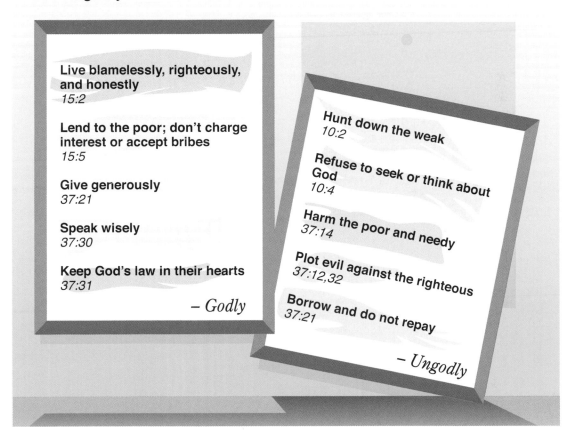

Live blamelessly, righteously, and honestly
15:2

Lend to the poor; don't charge interest or accept bribes
15:5

Give generously
37:21

Speak wisely
37:30

Keep God's law in their hearts
37:31

— Godly

Hunt down the weak
10:2

Refuse to seek or think about God
10:4

Harm the poor and needy
37:14

Plot evil against the righteous
37:12,32

Borrow and do not repay
37:21

— Ungodly

CROSS-REFERENCES

Psalm 1

Romans 6:15–18

Ephesians 4:17–24

CHAPTER 55

At one time or another, we've all felt like the author of Psalm 73. As he looked around one day at the "charmed" lives of godless people doing god-awful things, he had a mini faith crisis. Not until he remembered the destiny of the wicked did he recover. Here are some truths that can help us view such people and situations biblically:

God sees and knows. Proverbs 15:3 says unequivocally, "The eyes of the LORD are everywhere, keeping watch on the wicked and the good." Bottom line: There's no going "off the (spiritual) grid." We can't hide anything from God. All that sneaky stuff that evil people do in the shadows? None of it escapes God's notice.

God is patient. Why does God sometimes let evil go on for so long? Doesn't he care? Actually, he cares deeply—about the hearts of the unrighteous as well as the righteous. Speaking to those who suggested that maybe God would never judge evil, Peter wrote, "The Lord is . . . patient with you, not wanting anyone to perish, but everyone to come to repentance" (2 Peter 3:9). Don't miss that— God is patient with sinners.

God is gracious. God told the prophet Ezekiel to deliver a surprising message to Israelites bent on evil: "I take no pleasure in the death of the wicked, but rather that they turn from their ways and live. Turn! Turn from your evil ways! Why will you die, people of Israel?" (Ezekiel 33:11). Amazing! God wants to dole out favor— not punishment—to wicked people.

God is just. Those who continually spurn God's gracious overtures and reject the forgiveness available in Christ face a grim future indeed. Jesus said that everything done in the dark will one day be brought into the light (Luke 8:17). The apostle Paul warned, "Do not be deceived: God cannot be mocked. A man reaps what he sows" (Galatians 6:7). In other words, nobody ever gets away with anything.

The choice is simple: We can trust that Jesus was judged for our sins at the cross and experience the forgiveness and grace and mercy of God. Or we can decide to pay for our own sins and experience the severe (but fair) justice and wrath of God (Romans 5:9).

> Godless people might sometimes *seem* to live "charmed" lives. In truth they are headed for disaster. Don't wish evil on them, and don't gloat over their misfortune. Rather, pray for God's mercy to shatter their hard hearts and open their blind eyes.

PERSISTENT SIN

God will declare
their guilt
5:10

The trouble they
cause will come back
on them
7:16

Their schemes will
be their defeat
5:10

Consequences
for Evildoers

Psalms

They will be caught
in their own trap
7:15

They'll be banished
for their many sins
5:10

CROSS-REFERENCES

Psalm 37:1–2

Proverbs 5:22

2 Peter 2:17

CHAPTER 56

When people have a genuine encounter with God Almighty, shouldn't they be forever changed?

Take the ancient Israelites for example. The Bible records that they witnessed a string of undeniable miracles, culminating in their liberation from centuries of slavery in Egypt. Then, before they even had time to process all that, God parted the Red Sea, brought them to Mount Sinai, spoke audibly to them, then proceeded to feed and guide them supernaturally!

Such vivid experiences meant they never dishonored God again, right?

Wrong. As the infographic to the right shows, they doubted and disobeyed God constantly. Belief often gave way to unbelief. Obedience and disobedience often struggled in their hearts like two stray tomcats fighting in a burlap sack. If we charted the Israelites' spiritual experience, it would look like the EKG results of a person with a bad ticker. Regrettably, it would resemble our own up-and-down spiritual experience.

Three biblical truths to tuck away:

The enemy is always at work. Living in a way that honors God would be hard enough if we only had to battle our own wrong desires. But the Bible soberly warns of another enemy: Satan (aka the devil). And what a foe. He's a tempter and an accuser—and he excels in lurking, scheming, murdering, and lying.

We are in process. Consider how life works. Babies become toddlers, then move through childhood and adolescence into adulthood. At every stage (all the way to death), people make countless mistakes. This is also true in the spiritual realm. Coming to faith (Jesus called it being "born again"; see John 3) is the start, not the finish of a person's spiritual journey. We have to grow from spiritual infancy to maturity. Overall this journey is beautiful—day to day it's not always pretty.

God gives and forgives. The list of Bible men and women whose spiritual résumés include great victories *and* epic failures is long and illustrious. What this tells us is that our God is merciful. He knows us in our weakness and at our worst—and still he forgives. Even better, he gives us spiritual resources so that over time we can get better at loving and honoring God.

Life Application

It's easy to think that witnessing an undeniable miracle would solidify our faith. Did this happen with the Israelites during the time of Moses? In the time of Christ?

MISSTEPS IN HONORING GOD

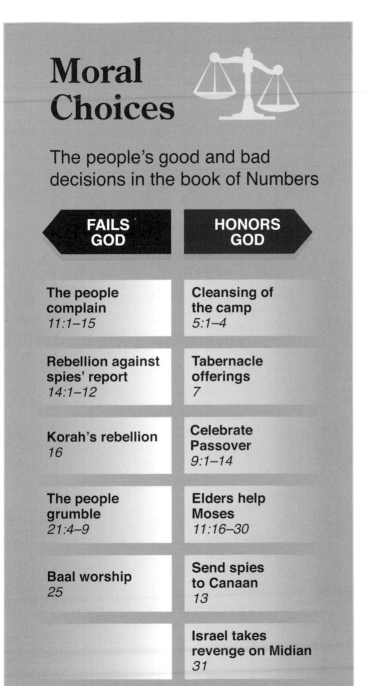

Moral Choices

The people's good and bad decisions in the book of Numbers

FAILS GOD	HONORS GOD
The people complain *11:1–15*	Cleansing of the camp *5:1–4*
Rebellion against spies' report *14:1–12*	Tabernacle offerings *7*
Korah's rebellion *16*	Celebrate Passover *9:1–14*
The people grumble *21:4–9*	Elders help Moses *11:16–30*
Baal worship *25*	Send spies to Canaan *13*
	Israel takes revenge on Midian *31*

SIN & THE SOLUTION

CROSS-REFERENCES

Exodus 24:3, 7; 32

1 Corinthians 3:1–2; 13:11; 14:20

1 Peter 2:2

CHAPTER 57

Some people are shocked at how "honest" the Bible is when highlighting its cast of characters—page after page is populated by doubters and hypocrites, womanizers and prostitutes, cowards and murderers. Even Abraham, the great patriarch of the faith, is shown to be a deeply flawed man.

What lessons can we learn from him (and from the Bible's other far-from-perfect people)?

1. Nobody has it all together. *Surely, we think, a saint like Abraham had God, faith, and the spiritual life all figured out, right?* Not even close. With the exception of Jesus (Hebrews 4:15), every human mentioned in Scripture (indeed, every person who has ever lived) is described as being sinful (Romans 3:23). Jacob, Moses, David, Solomon, Peter—they all had their issues. Read their stories.

2. Faith waxes and wanes. Abraham had moments when he demonstrated remarkable faith—like the day he obeyed God's call to leave his homeland (Genesis 12:1–5) and the day he offered up his beloved son Isaac (Genesis 22). But Abraham also had plenty of other moments marked by glaring doubt and disobedience (see the graphic to the right).

Abraham is not alone. The other characters of the Bible have similar spiritual résumés. Their experiences (and ours too) show that faith is never a static thing. It's fickle and fluid, strong some days and weak on others. When the flames of faith aren't stoked, it inevitably grows cold.

3. Although we are often faithless, God is always faithful. Despite Abraham's inconsistency, one thing never changed: God's loyal devotion to him. Read his story and note how God kept pursuing and protecting him, continually helping and blessing him. Maybe that's the biggest lesson we learn from the failures of Abraham. Rather than jeopardizing God's grace, our sins put his love and mercy on vivid display!

Life Application

Maybe you're one of those people who struggles with deep guilt. You have things in your rearview mirror—ugly secrets in your past—that you're convinced God can't forgive. Instead of focusing on all that you've done wrong, how about focusing on all that God did to make you right with him? Try reading Ephesians 1 and 2.

CROSS-REFERENCES
Romans 4
Galatians 3:6–9
Hebrews 11:8–12

IMPERFECT BIBLE HEROES

Abraham's Faults
Genesis 12–20

Though Abraham is known as the father of faith, he wasn't perfect; the Bible lists a number of faults that offer a glimpse into his human frailty:

Asks Sarah to lie and say she is his sister, thereby allowing her to be taken into Pharaoh's harem
12:11–13

Doesn't trust God to provide an heir through Sarah, so he sleeps with her Egyptian slave (Hagar) to produce one
16:1–4

Laughs when God promises he and Sarah will have a son
17:15–17

Again lies and says Sarah is his sister, allowing her to be taken into King Abimelek's harem
20:1–5

CHAPTER 58

It's interesting how life's worst moments can actually provide good inspiration.

You know this from experience. You witness someone fail in a very public and painful way. If you're compassionate, you say a prayer and offer help. But if you're wise, you also make some mental notes. *By God's grace, I won't do that thing. I will make different choices in my life.*

Thankfully, the Bible gives us a front-row seat to all the lives of its characters. We get to see them at their best and their worst. In the pages of Scripture, we find excellent role models and cautionary tales too. David's family, sadly, was an example of the latter.

As the graphic shows, three of David's sons were tragic figures. Amnon was consumed with lust. Absalom had anger issues and insatiable ambition. Adonijah was envious, conniving, and prideful.

Are we really surprised? David, the father of these men—despite his love for God—had engaged in a scandalous affair (2 Samuel 11) and had the woman's husband, one of his best generals, killed. What's more, David had collected wives (2 Samuel 5:13) like some millionaires collect classic cars. Then, perhaps because he got so busy trying both to rule a kingdom and keep all those spouses happy, David was too distracted (and/or tired) to confront his sons' misbehavior (2 Samuel 13–14).

The story serves as a sobering picture of how wrong thoughts lead to wrong actions, and how wrong actions lead to devastation. All three sons died brutally. David was left to think about what might have been, a blubbering monarch filled with regret (2 Samuel 18–19).

A different son of David—one from his mistress-turned-wife Bathsheba—succeeded David as king. Thinking about sin and its consequences—perhaps remembering his own dysfunctional family and all those dead half brothers—Solomon wisely cautioned, "There is a way that appears to be right, but in the end it leads to death" (Proverbs 14:12).

That's as good a warning—and summary of sin—as we'll ever find.

Life Application

Spend a few minutes thinking about some specific times in your life when you saw the sobering truth of Proverbs 14:12 rear its head in the life of someone you love.

LEARNING FROM DAVID'S TROUBLED SONS

SIN & THE SOLUTION

Troubled Sons of David

DAVID

Amnon	Absalom	Adonijah
▸ Rapes his sister Tamar ▸ Killed by Absalom *2Sa 13*	▸ Kills his brother Amnon for raping their sister Tamar ▸ Revolts against David ▸ Killed in war of rebellion against David *2Sa 13:22–39; 15; 18*	▸ Tries to make himself king instead of Solomon ▸ Killed after he asks Solomon for David's concubine *1Ki 1; 2:13–25*

CROSS-REFERENCES

Psalms 25; 51

Daniel 9:9

CHAPTER 59

SIN & THE SOLUTION

By any standard or definition, Jesus was extraordinary. The Gospels show him feeding the hungry, healing the sick, freeing the demon-possessed, walking on water, and resurrecting the dead! Amid all these eye-popping miracles, another common activity of Jesus often gets lost: forgiving sinners.

Jesus claimed the authority to forgive sin. When Jesus told a paralytic that his sins were forgiven (Luke 5:17–26), the Jewish religious leaders standing nearby were appalled. *Who can forgive sins but God alone?* they wondered. *This is blasphemy!* Here was a not-so-subtle claim of deity on the part of Jesus, the carpenter-turned-teacher from Nazareth. Then, as if to "prove" his words, he healed the man.

Jesus viewed forgiveness as our biggest need of all. The world would look at a paralytic and say his biggest need is physical healing. Jesus saw a deeper need: healing the man's heart. Forgiveness is the greatest gift of God because it brings permanent spiritual healing. Consider that every person whom Jesus healed (physically) in the Gospels eventually died. Yet the people he forgave were given new, spiritual life that will never end.

Jesus forgave people whom religious society viewed with disgust and disdain. Jesus extended forgiveness to people with ugly pasts and messy "presents" (Luke 7:44–48; John 4). He forgave a man who stole a lot of money (Luke 19:1–10). He forgave a woman who had sex with another woman's spouse (John 8:1–11). He was even forgiving to his executioners (Luke 23:34). Always Jesus forgave unconditionally. He never demanded that people "clean up their acts" before making promises like "Today you will be with me in paradise" (Luke 23:43).

Jesus forgave people who should have known better. For about three years, Peter had a front-row seat to the phenomenal life of Jesus. What's more, he was one of Jesus' closest friends! Yet when Jesus was arrested, Peter's faith gave way to fear. He denied even knowing Christ. This betrayal had to wound Jesus to the heart, yet he showed stunning grace to Peter. He forgave him and reiterated his desire for Peter to take the gospel to the world (John 21:15–19).

Two things are true:

1. No matter what you've done, Jesus stands ready to forgive you.
2. No matter what's been done to you, Jesus stands ready to help you forgive. "Bear with each other and forgive one another if any of you has a grievance against someone. Forgive as the Lord forgave you" (Colossians 3:13).

THE EXTENT OF JESUS' FORGIVENESS

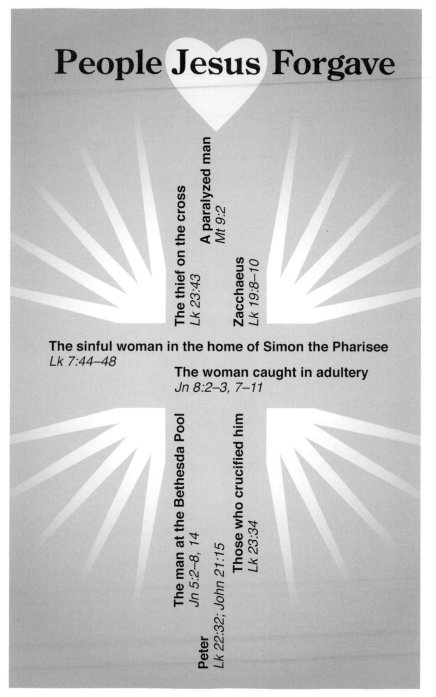

People Jesus Forgave

The thief on the cross
Lk 23:43

A paralyzed man
Mt 9:2

Zacchaeus
Lk 19:8–10

The sinful woman in the home of Simon the Pharisee
Lk 7:44–48

The woman caught in adultery
Jn 8:2–3, 7–11

The man at the Bethesda Pool
Jn 5:2–8, 14

Those who crucified him
Lk 23:34

Peter
Lk 22:32; John 21:15

CROSS-REFERENCES

Psalm 103:3

Acts 13:38

Ephesians 1:7

PART 9

LIVING AS A CHRISTIAN

CHAPTER 60

Physically, humans need food and water, shelter and rest. But emotionally and spiritually we need so much more. If you've ever felt unloved or excluded, you know how important it is to belong, to feel accepted and loved. Likewise, when we feel unsafe or insignificant, life becomes almost unbearable.

The message of Jesus is truly "good news" in that it meets all these essential needs—and then some.

In Christ we find ultimate *acceptance.* Before trusting Christ, we were God's enemies (Romans 5:10), but Jesus—through his death—made it possible for us to be reconciled to our Maker. In Christ, God forgives—fully and forever—*all* our sins (Colossians 1:13–14). The Bible further speaks of how God chooses us and adopts us into his family (Ephesians 1:3–8). By faith we actually become God's beloved children (John 1:12) and heirs (Romans 8:17). Jesus even calls his followers "friends" (John 15:15). What's more, he gives us 24/7 access to God's throne of grace (Hebrews 4:14–16).

In Christ we experience ultimate *security.* It's a scary world, but Christians are the safest people on the planet. Consider these truths: We are forever free from divine condemnation (Romans 8:1–2), and nothing anywhere can ever separate us from the love of God (Romans 8:31–39). We are born of God, and the Evil One cannot touch us

> While writing his letter to the Romans, the apostle Paul abruptly broke into praise over God's hard-to-fathom grace. He wrote:
>
> *Oh, the depth of the riches of the*
>   *wisdom and knowledge of God!*
> *How unsearchable his judgments,*
>   *and his paths beyond tracing out!*
> *"Who has known the mind of the Lord?*
>   *Or who has been his counselor?"*
> *"Who has ever given to God,*
>   *that God should repay them?"*
> *For from him and through him and for*
>   *him are all things.*
> *To him be the glory forever! Amen.*
>
> Romans 11:33–36

(1 John 5:18). We have heavenly citizenship (Philippians 3:20) and the promise that God will finish the good work he has started in us (Philippians 1:6).

In Christ we discover ultimate *purpose.* The life of a Christian is anything but random and meaningless. We're not just killing time until we die. According to Scripture, each believer is a one-of-a-kind masterpiece created for good works (Ephesians 2:10). Not only this, but we've been given at least

A CHRISTIAN'S NEW IDENTITY

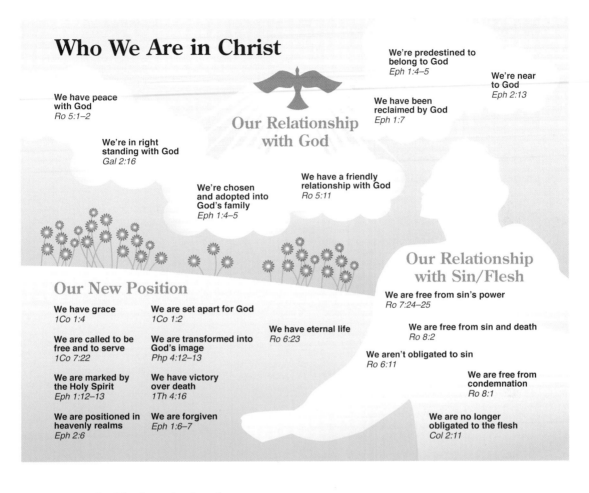

Who We Are in Christ

We're predestined to belong to God
Eph 1:4–5

We're near to God
Eph 2:13

We have peace with God
Ro 5:1–2

Our Relationship with God

We have been reclaimed by God
Eph 1:7

We're in right standing with God
Gal 2:16

We're chosen and adopted into God's family
Eph 1:4–5

We have a friendly relationship with God
Ro 5:11

Our New Position

We have grace
1Co 1:4

We are set apart for God
1Co 1:2

We are called to be free and to serve
1Co 7:22

We are transformed into God's image
Php 4:12–13

We have eternal life
Ro 6:23

We are marked by the Holy Spirit
Eph 1:12–13

We have victory over death
1Th 4:16

We are positioned in heavenly realms
Eph 2:6

We are forgiven
Eph 1:6–7

Our Relationship with Sin/Flesh

We are free from sin's power
Ro 7:24–25

We are free from sin and death
Ro 8:2

We aren't obligated to sin
Ro 6:11

We are free from condemnation
Ro 8:1

We are no longer obligated to the flesh
Col 2:11

one spiritual gift that the Lord wants us to use to grow and strengthen his church (Ephesians 4:16; 1 Peter 4:10). Furthermore, we're God's ambassadors, appointed to represent him to this world (2 Corinthians 5:19–21). We can do that and bear spiritual fruit for God (John 15:16) because his Holy Spirit lives inside us (1 Corinthians 6:19) to empower us to take his good news to the world (Acts 1:8).

CROSS-REFERENCES

Romans 5:1

Philippians 4:13

Colossians 2:9–10

CHAPTER 61

The Bible is alive (Hebrews 4:12). With penetrating power it reveals what God is like. What's more, it tells the amazing story of all that God did to bring sinners into right relationship with himself through Jesus Christ. The Bible heals, comforts, transforms, guides, and more.

Obviously, we'd be foolish not to read a book like that, but *how* should we read? Here are ten ways:

1. **Prayerfully.** With the psalmist, ask the Lord, "Open my eyes that I may see wonderful things in your law" (Psalm 119:18).
2. **Warily.** Never forget that Satan is an expert truth-snatcher (Mark 4:15) and truth-distorter (Matthew 4:1–11). Be mindful of his devilish schemes as you read.
3. **Hungrily.** As a baby wants, needs, and thrives on milk (1 Peter 2:2), look to God's Word for nourishment—and not just occasionally.
4. **Daily.** Be like the wise Bereans (Acts 17:11) who examined the Scriptures *every day*.
5. **Attentively.** When Nehemiah read the Book of the Law to the ancient people of God, they "listened attentively" (Nehemiah 8:3).
6. **Objectively.** It's easy to bring presuppositions, biases, and personal agendas to the Bible. It's also dangerous. Proverbs 30:6 warns against adding to God's words. We need to be careful that we don't start "seeing" things in the text that aren't there.
7. **Submissively/humbly.** James urges believers to "humbly accept the word planted in you, which can save you" (James 1:21). This means embracing a "yes" mindset when reading God's Word.
8. **Completely.** Beware of the tendency to develop a favorite chapter/book/ testament and "camp out" there. *"All Scripture is God-breathed and is useful for teaching, rebuking, correcting and training in righteousness"* (2 Timothy 3:16, emphasis added).
9. **Expectantly.** Young Samuel was encouraged to pray, "Speak, LORD, for your servant is listening," and then to wait (1 Samuel 3:9). As we read, we should believe the astonishing truth that God wants to reveal himself and his will to us.
10. **Lovingly.** "Oh, how I love your law!" the psalmist cried (Psalm 119:97). The Bible is a priceless gift of grace, a treasure chest of wisdom, and a lamp in a dark world.

CROSS-REFERENCES

Psalm 119

Isaiah 40:8

Romans 15:4

BIBLE READING

Why Read the Bible?

The Bible is the bestselling book of all time and continues to sell millions of copies every year. People turn to the Bible for many different reasons, but its primary purpose is to deliver a message—God's message. Below are four truths that attest to why the Bible's life-giving words are worth reading.

The Bible . . .

Reveals God's Son, Jesus Christ, who experienced death on the cross to pay the penalty for humanity's sins
Jn 20:31

Evidence for the Truth

■ Christ's life and ministry are prophesied in the opening chapter of Genesis and culminate with great promise and hope for people in the last chapter of Revelation

The Bible . . .

Is inspired by God and is without error
2 Tim. 3:16–17

Evidence for the Truth

■ Was miraculously written over the course of 1,500 years by more than 40 different writers

■ Contains hundreds of prophecies that have been fulfilled

■ Is consistently proven historically accurate through archaeological finds

■ Is indestructible—has survived being banned, burned and confiscated

The Bible . . .

Changes lives
Heb 4:12

Evidence for the Truth

■ Convicts people of their sin

■ Inspires people to love God and others

■ Compels people to risk their lives to protect it

The Bible . . .

Delivers God's truth in ways people can understand
Ac 17:11; Rom. 12:2; 2 Cor. 10:5; Col. 3:16; 2 Tim. 2:15

Evidence for the Truth

■ Helps readers to mature

■ Renews minds

■ Directs thoughts to Christ

■ Gives wisdom

CHAPTER 62

What was humanity's original sin? Simply put, it was the refusal to trust God's heart and believe his Word. This gross unbelief led to a shocking act of rebellion.

God's gracious response was to send Jesus to pay for mankind's sin—and to call unbelievers everywhere to trust in him for forgiveness and new life.

In short, unbelief leads to death. Faith in Jesus alone brings life—eternal "life . . . to the full" (John 10:10).

With so much confusion about faith, we need to remember some basic truths:

Faith is essential. Apart from faith, we cannot be right with God (Romans 5:1; Philippians 3:9), nor can we please God (Hebrews 11:6). Faith is the only way we can come alive spiritually, and it's how we're called to live for the entirety of our lives (Philippians 1:6).

Faith is not simply an intellectual exercise. Biblical faith is more than just knowing biblical truths. James said that even demons nod at right theology (James 2:19). Genuine faith always prompts a response—in other words, faith is more verb than noun. James spoke of the necessity of demonstrating our faith by our works (James 2:14–26). Hebrews 11, the great faith chapter in the Bible, shows people taking (often risky) *steps* of faith, not merely speaking *words* of faith.

Faith is fluid, not fixed. Just because our faith was strong yesterday doesn't mean it will never falter. The Bible is filled with great heroes of the faith who had moments of doubt or even seasons when their faith flickered and sputtered. Thankfully, the promise of the Bible is that "if we are faithless, he remains faithful" (2 Timothy 2:13). Ultimately it's *where* our faith rests—that is, in Jesus—not *how much* faith we possess (or how intense it happens to be) that matters most to God.

Faith can grow. Speaking of Abraham, Romans 4:20 mentions how "with respect to the promise of God, he did not waver in unbelief but *grew strong in faith*."

Life Application

How can you develop stronger faith? Three suggestions: First, pray the same prayer the disciples prayed: "Increase our faith!" (Luke 17:5). Second, spend time reading, studying, and memorizing God's Word— because "faith comes from hearing the message" (Romans 10:17). Third, when you doubt, don't despair. Rather, say to the Lord, "Help me overcome my unbelief!" (Mark 9:24).

A LEAP OF FAITH

What Is Faith?

Faith is one of the central parts of our relationship with God. Faith in God is tested daily—by terrible news stories, by personal troubles, by the human failings of family and friends—and yet the more we live by our faith, the better we are able to make our way in the world by trusting in God and his ultimate plan for the human race.

Mt 17:20

COMPONENTS OF FAITH IN GOD	WHAT THIS MEANS FOR US
1. Belief in the existence of God and his unseen kingdom *Heb 11:1–40*	■ HOPE—We can look forward to a world beyond this one where we will live in peace with God forever ■ ACTION—If we truly believe there is more to life than what can be seen, our faith will drive our values and actions to align with our belief
2. Belief that the world and everything in it is part of God's plan and under his control *Mt 17:20; Jn 1:3*	■ MEANING TO LIFE—Those with faith know that everything that happens to them is for a purpose and is part of a greater plan ■ POWER—Even the smallest amount of faith can change lives and help us through times of troubles
3. Belief in the Bible as the objective Word of God *Ps 33:4; 119:105; Ro 10:17; Col 1:10; 1Th 2:13*	■ GUIDANCE—The Bible provides guidance for living every day by faith ■ APPROVAL—God is pleased when we grow in our faith and knowledge of him by reading the Bible

CROSS-REFERENCES

Habakkuk 2:4

John 6:28–29

1 John 5:4

CHAPTER 63

If we're like most spiritually minded people, we've probably noticed times when our faith is solid and real, and other times when it feels very shaky and suspect. Or perhaps we've noticed that while others appear to be making great strides in their faith, we seem stuck. What does the Bible say about *growing in faith*?

With almost five hundred mentions of *faith* (plus hundreds of other references to trust, reliance on God, etc.), the Bible is all about faith—and about the many means God uses to spark and grow authentic faith in our hearts. Here are four:

Grace. Ephesians 2:8–9 says that salvation comes to us "by grace . . . through faith." In other words, the Lord graciously initiates spiritual life and growth. He is the source, the "pioneer and perfecter of faith" (Hebrews 12:2). If we want a growing faith, he's where we have to go.

Relationships. Once, when writing a letter to Christians he'd never met, the apostle Paul expressed his hope that he might be able one day to be with them in person. Why? So that "you and I may be mutually encouraged by each other's faith" (Romans 1:12). It's a fact: when believers who are serious about living by faith spend time together, they rub off on each other in good ways. They spur each other on to deeper faith (Hebrews 10:24–25).

Opportunities to trust and serve. Life is full of difficult circumstances. Instead of despairing, however, we can be joyful in tough times (James 1:2). How? By turning to God and watching him bring good out of bad. Suppose a trial happens to a friend. That is a chance to step forward. As we support our hurting friend, we trust that God's love will flow through us. In short, hardships—whether personal or affecting someone close to us—offer opportunities to (a) see God work and (b) see faith grow.

Word of God. Paul famously said, "Faith comes from hearing the message, and the message is heard through the word about Christ" (Romans 10:17). The better we know the Bible, the better we know the One who is the author and main character of the Bible. His trustworthy character fosters trust.

Life Application

If your faith is shaky or small, ask God to help you grow in your trust. Pray the great prayer of the disciples in Luke 17:5.

GROWING IN FAITH

Growing in Faith

Genesis 12–24

Abraham is often referred to as the "father of faith" because of the many striking times he places his full trust in God and his plan

Examples of Abraham's Faith in Scripture

1 Travels from his home in Harran to Canaan as God instructed him
12:1–5

2 Builds two altars in response to God's promise to give the land to his offspring
12:7–8

3 Allows Lot first choice of the land
13:5–9

4 Goes to war to rescue Lot
14:11–16

5 Gives Melchizedek a tenth of all the spoils *14:18–20*

6 Believes God when he promises him numerous offspring *15:4–6*

7 Obeys God's command to circumcise the males of his household and undergo circumcision himself
17:23–27

8 Prepares food for the Lord and his angels *18:1–8*

9 Pleads on behalf of the righteous people in Sodom and Gomorrah
18:16–33

10 Sends Hagar and Ishmael away per God's instruction that he listen to Sarah
21:9–14

11 Is willing to sacrifice Isaac *22:1–18*

12 Sends his servant to find Isaac a wife among his relatives
24:1–61

CROSS-REFERENCES

Proverbs 3:5–6

Mark 9:14–27

Hebrews 11

CHAPTER 64

Before we discuss the question "Why go to church?" perhaps we need to ask and answer, "What *is* the church?"

Contrary to popular belief, church isn't a building. The New Testament word translated "church" (the Greek word *ekklesia*) literally means "called-out ones." Thus, the Bible uses the word *church* to speak of (a) all believers in Christ everywhere (1 Corinthians 12:28) and (b) individual congregations in specific locales (1 Corinthians 1:2). The crucial truth? The church isn't a place; it's *people*—a global community (made up of local assemblies) of those who share a common faith in Christ.

This distinction answers the question "Why go to church?" *Because we were never meant to do life alone* (Genesis 2:18). We need to be connected to others who are seeking to know and love and serve God! This can mean worshiping together (in an actual "church facility" on Sundays). But technically church also "happens" whenever we gather with other believers—for lunch on Thursday or for prayer on Friday mornings before work.

We pursue Christ alongside other believers because the church is the only entity on earth that Jesus committed to build and bless (Matthew 16:18). We become part of a Christian community to use our spiritual gifts to build up the body of Christ (1 Peter 4:10), and God uses other believers to help us grow (Romans 12:3–8). We must not ignore the truth that the Bible explicitly tells believers not to give up "meeting together, as some are in the habit of doing" (Hebrews 10:25).

The church is the "bride of Christ." Interestingly, ancient biblical congregations are marked by four qualities we can remember using the acrostic WIFE:

Worship—the glory of God being central (1 Corinthians 10:31)

Instruction—the Word of God being taught boldly and lived out faithfully (2 Timothy 3:16–17)

Fellowship—members sharing life and resources as they engage in a common mission together (Acts 2:42–47)

Evangelism—the priority being to make disciples of all nations (Matthew 28:18–20)

Life Application

Pray that your congregation would follow the biblical blueprint (WIFE), and do your part to help it become that kind of faith family.

If you aren't part of a good church, ask God to lead you to a healthy spiritual community.

WHY CHURCH?

Why Go to Church?

In this era of celebrated individuality, many people believe that organized religion—church—is an outdated concept that doesn't work for today's individual. However, participating in corporate worship is considerably valuable for a Christian's spiritual growth. Jesus Christ established his church as a community of his followers who gather to celebrate God, encourage one another and spread the Good News. It is important to understand what the church is in order to understand the benefits of being a part of it.

The church Is . . .

THE BRIDE OF CHRIST
Jn 17:20–26;
Eph 5:25–27;
Rev 19:7; 21:9

THE BODY OF CHRIST
Ro 12:3–8; 1Co 12:12–31;
Eph 4:11–16

A PLACE FOR GROWTH
Ro 1:12; Eph 4:29;
Col 3:13; 1Th 5:11;
2Th 1:3

Benefits

- We, the collective followers of Jesus Christ (his bride), are the object of his affection and glory
- Christ's relationship with his church is permanent
- The world can know God's love through the unity of believers and their commitment to Christ

- The church brings God's people together; Christ is the spiritual "head" that connects and directs them
- Serving others within a church community allows us to use our God-given gifts
- When we serve each other, we embody the message of God's love, just as Jesus embodied God himself
- God provides unity for his people to ensure that we are never alone, even in times of need

- The church is a community of people who are accepted and forgiven
- We as believers rely on each other to increase in our faith and commitment to Christ
- We build each other up through love and service
- By working together, we work toward the benefit of each other

CROSS-REFERENCES

Colossians 3:12–17

1 Peter 2:9–10

CHAPTER 65

Med school students take a course in gross anatomy. It's gross all right—the class involves a cadaver and lots of dissecting. And yet most come away marveling at the incredible intricacies of the human body. No wonder the Spirit of God prompted the apostle Paul to use the metaphor of a human body as a picture of how Jesus designed his church to function.

Here's what the biblical teaching about the body of Christ shows us:

Faith is a "we" thing, not a "me" thing. Nowhere does the Bible advocate an individualized spirituality. "One body with many members" (Romans 12:4) is how Paul put it. He went on to say, "Just as a body, though one, has many parts, but all its many parts form one body, so it is with Christ" (v. 5). In other words, like it or not, we're connected. "The body is a unit . . . made up of many parts" (1 Corinthians 12:12). The famed Swiss psychiatrist Paul Tournier said it well: "There are two things we cannot do alone: one is to be married and the other is to be a Christian."

We are called to function interdependently, not independently. The New Testament makes it clear that God has intentionally designed each one of us with certain strengths and definite limitations. This is so that we will need one another.

"The eye cannot say to the hand, 'I don't need you!'" (1 Corinthians 12:21). Anybody who has ever had a stray eyelash in the old peeper knows that a steady hand is, well, handy. Sometimes the eye needs a hand. Sometimes the hand needs an eye.

We're each "indispensable." In the world, it's typically the star actor who gets the accolades, the hotshot quarterback who is named MVP, and the high-profile CEO who gets the whopping bonus. But where would any of them be without their crew, team, or sales force? Paul made it clear that in the church, things are radically different. From God's point of view, every Christian is vital and each one's role is hugely significant. Paul insisted, "Those parts of the body that seem to be weaker are indispensable" (1 Corinthians 12:22).

Life Application

Look around. More and more people seem to view faith as a private matter. St. John of the Cross warned about this kind of solitary spirituality: "The virtuous soul that is alone . . . is like the burning coal that is alone. It will grow colder rather than hotter." Do you think he was right?

THE BODY OF CHRIST

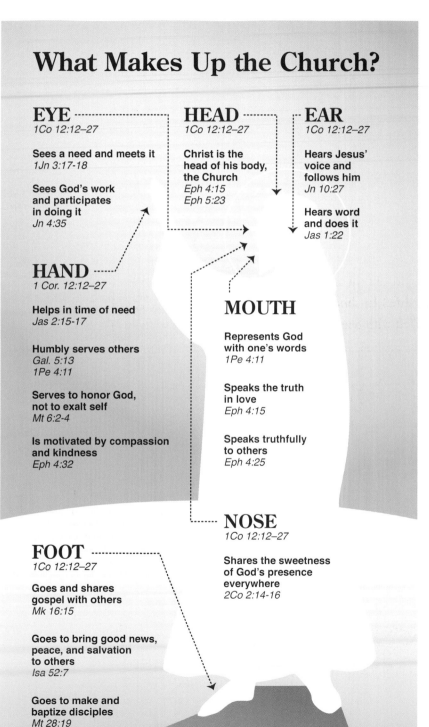

What Makes Up the Church?

EYE
1Co 12:12–27

Sees a need and meets it
1Jn 3:17-18

Sees God's work
and participates
in doing it
Jn 4:35

HAND
1 Cor. 12:12–27

Helps in time of need
Jas 2:15-17

Humbly serves others
Gal. 5:13
1Pe 4:11

Serves to honor God,
not to exalt self
Mt 6:2-4

Is motivated by compassion
and kindness
Eph 4:32

HEAD
1Co 12:12–27

Christ is the
head of his body,
the Church
Eph 4:15
Eph 5:23

EAR
1Co 12:12–27

Hears Jesus'
voice and
follows him
Jn 10:27

Hears word
and does it
Jas 1:22

MOUTH

Represents God
with one's words
1Pe 4:11

Speaks the truth
in love
Eph 4:15

Speaks truthfully
to others
Eph 4:25

NOSE
1Co 12:12–27

Shares the sweetness
of God's presence
everywhere
2Co 2:14-16

FOOT
1Co 12:12–27

Goes and shares
gospel with others
Mk 16:15

Goes to bring good news,
peace, and salvation
to others
Isa 52:7

Goes to make and
baptize disciples
Mt 28:19

CROSS-REFERENCES

Matthew 16:15–18

Hebrews 10:24–25

1 Peter 4:7–11

CHAPTER 66

Think of all the things a person can be at once—child, sibling, grandchild, spouse, parent, niece, cousin, friend, student, homeowner, neighbor, taxpaying citizen, employee . . . and on and on.

When the Bible speaks of the modern-day people of God, it doesn't simply call us "believers." Rather, it identifies us using a broad array of picturesque terms and phrases. Each one of these descriptors says something powerful about our true spiritual identity and about the One who names us.

The Lord is *for* us. The fact that the Lord loves (Romans 8:38–39) and accepts us (Romans 15:7), chooses (Ephesians 1:4) and forgives us (Ephesians 1:6–8), should tell us all we need to know. But the descriptions don't stop there. The Bible says that God adopts us into his family (Romans 8:14–16) to be his "heirs" (Romans 8:17) and calls us his "handiwork" (Ephesians 2:10). Altogether, as part of the church, Christians comprise "the bride of Christ" (Revelation 19:7). We are precious to God. No wonder one translation of Exodus 19:5 refers to the ancient people of God as his "treasured possession."

The Lord is *with* us. One of the verses we often hear during the Christmas season is Matthew 1:23: "'The virgin will conceive and give birth to a son, and they will call him Immanuel' (which means 'God with us')." The picture of God entering his creation—being with us—is a powerful image. It's echoed in John 1:14, which says that Jesus "made his dwelling among us."

Although God has always been with his creation, he offered tangible proof that he cared so deeply that he revealed himself through the incarnation of Jesus. While living in human form, Jesus turned to those who identified with him and encouraged them to follow him (Mark 8:34–38). God's desire to be with us became a tangible picture of Jesus walking alongside his followers. And rather than leave them alone after his ascension, he revealed that he is the head of the community where Christians continue to gather: the church (1 Corinthians 12). Christ remains the head because he continues to live with us. We do not labor alone. We do not walk without him. We do not worship in isolation. Through it all, he continues to show a connection and union with his people.

The Lord works *through* us. Many of these believer descriptions—for example, fruit-bearing branches (John 15:2–6), ambassadors (2 Corinthians 5:20), light (Matthew 5:14)—clearly show how God wants to use us to make an eternal difference in the world.

GOD'S RELATIONSHIP WITH BELIEVERS

Descriptions of Believers and the Church

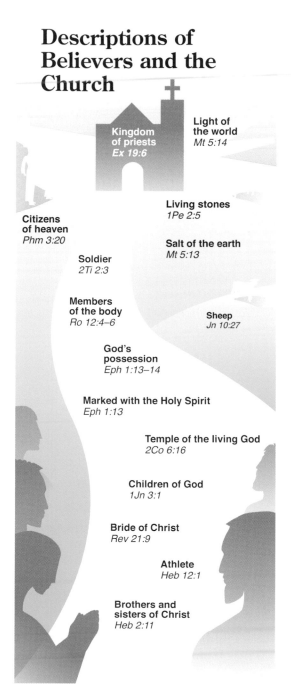

Kingdom of priests
Ex 19:6

Light of the world
Mt 5:14

Citizens of heaven
Phm 3:20

Living stones
1Pe 2:5

Salt of the earth
Mt 5:13

Soldier
2Ti 2:3

Members of the body
Ro 12:4–6

Sheep
Jn 10:27

God's possession
Eph 1:13–14

Marked with the Holy Spirit
Eph 1:13

Temple of the living God
2Co 6:16

Children of God
1Jn 3:1

Bride of Christ
Rev 21:9

Athlete
Heb 12:1

Brothers and sisters of Christ
Heb 2:11

The name "Christian" is found only three times in the Bible (Acts 11:26; 26:28; 1 Peter 4:16). Some scholars think that devotees of other religions used this term as a derogatory way of referring to followers of Jesus. The most common label for Christ-followers in the New Testament? "Disciple"—which means "student" or "learner."

CROSS-REFERENCES

Matthew 10:16

2 Timothy 2:5

1 Peter 2:11

CHAPTER 67

Depending on how we define the phrase "Bible promise," and depending on who's counting, there are somewhere between two thousand and eight thousand promises in the Bible. No wonder this topic raises so many questions.

What's a Bible promise? In the strictest sense, a Bible promise is a pledge by God that he will or will not do a certain thing. With the giving of such an assurance, a believer in God has every right to expect God to keep his word.

Is every Bible promise for everybody? Clearly not. Many of the divine promises in Scripture were given to specific individuals or people in historically unique situations. For example, God's pledge to give Abraham and Sarah a son in their old age (Genesis 12:1; 15:1–6; 18:10) doesn't mean that God promises every infertile couple a male heir.

Or take 2 Chronicles 7:14, which says, "If my people, who are called by my name, will humble themselves and pray and seek my face and turn from their wicked ways, then I will hear from heaven, and I will forgive their sin and will heal their land." Technically, this was a pledge given by God to ancient Israel at the dedication of Solomon's temple. It's *not* an iron-clad promise to send national revival to modern-day believers who faithfully hold prayer meetings (though of course the verse does contain truth that is reiterated in the New Testament: God hears and responds to humble prayers for forgiveness; see 1 John 1:9).

Are all Bible promises for here and now? No. Some promises have already been fulfilled in history—for example, God's repeated Old Testament promise to send a Messiah (i.e., a Savior-King; see Deuteronomy 18:15–19). Other divine pledges (like the promises to bestow rewards and transform believers into Christlikeness; see Romans 8:29; 2 Corinthians 3:18; 1 John 3:2) won't be fully realized until the life to come.

Is it wrong to "claim" a Bible promise? It is always right to "stand on God's promises." It's fitting to trust our trustworthy God. We should always believe that he will do everything he has promised to do. On the other hand, it is wrong to enter the presence of God with a demanding, "hurry up!" attitude. God is our King, and his timetable is often very different than ours. Therefore we must always maintain a spirit of humility and patience.

When we read the Bible's promises like the ones described above, it's best to look at the principle behind the biblical statement and examine what we can learn about the character of God from the promise. While the promise itself may not apply to us, the character of God is unchanging, and the things he valued then are things he still values.

GOD'S PROMISES

God's Promises to Christians

Heaven
Jn 14:2

An inheritance
Col 3:23–24

Eternal life
Jn 3:16

Treasure in heaven
Mt 19:21

A crown
1Co 9:24–25

A prize
Php 3:13–14

> *God never made a promise that was too good to be true.*
> D. L. Moody

CROSS-REFERENCES

Isaiah 26:3

Luke 6:35

James 1:5

CHAPTER 68

A spiritual gift is a supernatural ability God gives a believer for building up the church, the body of Christ. We get our theological understanding of spiritual gifts primarily from four key passages found in four New Testament epistles: Romans 12, 1 Corinthians 12, Ephesians 4, and 1 Peter 4.

Some Christians think the gifts mentioned in these four passages do not include every spiritual gift given by God. For example, they consider "singleness" (Matthew 19:10–12; 1 Corinthians 7:32) and "craftsmanship" (Exodus 31:1–11) as spiritual gifts.

Other Christians believe that certain spiritual gifts were temporary in nature (i.e., given to authenticate the apostles' message up until the writing of the New Testament). Typically, it is the "sign gifts" (healing, miraculous powers, prophecy, speaking in / interpreting tongues) and apostleship they view in this way.

Gifts are distributed to Christians by the Spirit of God as he sovereignly wills (1 Corinthians 12:11, 18). They are bestowed on the basis of grace—not merit (1 Corinthians 12:4–6, 11). This means no one should ever be prideful or embarrassed as a result of their gifting.

Every follower of Jesus has at least one gift (1 Corinthians 12:7; Ephesians 4:7), but only the entire body of Christ possesses every gift.

For the body of Christ (i.e., the church) to function as God intended, each believer must employ his or her gift (1 Peter 4:10).

Life Application

- While God gives some Christians supernatural ability to serve, give, show mercy, or share the gospel, it's important to remember that the New Testament commands *all* believers to engage in these particular ministries. Therefore, in these areas, no one can use the excuse, "Sorry, God never gave me that gift!"

- You can prayerfully discern your spiritual gifts in one or more of the following ways: *evaluation* (thinking back over your spiritual experience—i.e., what ministry was positive and what wasn't), *experimentation* (volunteering for assorted service opportunities), *effectiveness* (noting where God uses you most powerfully), *enjoyment* (considering the type of ministry efforts that make you come alive with gladness), and/or *examination* (taking an online spiritual gifts assessment).

CROSS-REFERENCES

Joel 2:28

Acts 1:8; 11:24; 13:52

SERVING GOD WITH SPIRITUAL GIFTS

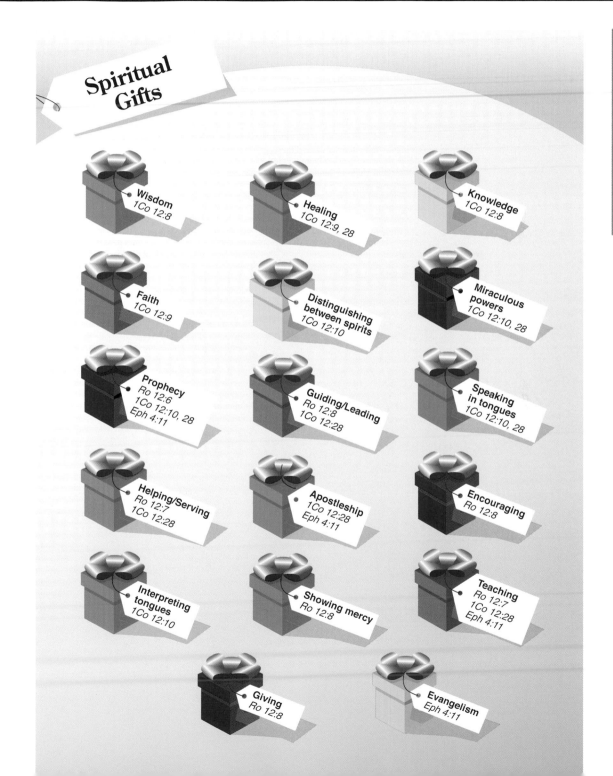

Spiritual Gifts

Wisdom
1Co 12:8

Healing
1Co 12:9, 28

Knowledge
1Co 12:8

Faith
1Co 12:9

Distinguishing between spirits
1Co 12:10

Miraculous powers
1Co 12:10, 28

Prophecy
Ro 12:6
1Co 12:10, 28
Eph 4:11

Guiding/Leading
Ro 12:8
1Co 12:28

Speaking in tongues
1Co 12:10, 28

Helping/Serving
Ro 12:7
1Co 12:28

Apostleship
1Co 12:28
Eph 4:11

Encouraging
Ro 12:8

Interpreting tongues
1Co 12:10

Showing mercy
Ro 12:8

Teaching
Ro 12:7
1Co 12:28
Eph 4:11

Giving
Ro 12:8

Evangelism
Eph 4:11

CHAPTER 69

The New Testament tells of the life, death, and resurrection of Christ and the birth and growth of the Christian church. Its twenty-seven books are said to contain around 800 unique commands for Christians. (Compare this to the Old Testament Mosaic law, which contains a mere 613 commands!)

That's a *lot* of instructions to remember and obey, which is no doubt why Jesus promised to send a Helper (i.e., the Holy Spirit; see John 14:16; 16:7). It's perhaps also why he seemed to emphasize one command above the rest. On the night before his crucifixion, Jesus told his closest followers: "A new command I give you: Love one another. As I have loved you, so you must love one another" (John 13:34).

Clearly, love is paramount to Jesus. On another occasion, he summarized the whole Old Testament law by saying, in essence, "Love God and love people" (Mark 12:28–34).

Why is love such a big deal? Here's why: God's essential nature is love (1 John 4:7, 16). Therefore, Christians (i.e., those who are new creatures in Christ [2 Corinthians 5:17] and children of God [John 1:12]) ought to resemble their heavenly Father. After giving the command to love, Jesus added the reason why: "By this everyone will know that you are my disciples" (John 13:35). Love is the clearest proof that the gospel is true.

Conversely, believers' failure to love each other gives the watching world the right to question if we're truly followers of Jesus.

What does biblical love look like? Biblical love isn't mere talk and mushy sentiment. God's love is *active* (John 3:16; 1 John 3:17–18). In one sense, you could say all of those 800 New Testament commands are rooted in love. Jesus said that we show our love for him by obeying his commands (John 14:21). And all our interactions with others spring from love too. We forgive (Colossians 3:13) and honor other people (Romans 12:10) out of love. Kind and compassionate acts (Ephesians 4:32), acts of service (Galatians 5:13), and hospitality (1 Peter 4:9)—all these are fruits of love.

It's also love that restrains us from wrong: *I can't slander him* (James 4:11), or *How could I dare pass judgment on her?* (Romans 14:13), we think. *God doesn't treat me that way.* Peter must have been listening to his Master's emphasis on love. He concluded, "Above all, love each other deeply, because love covers over a multitude of sins" (1 Peter 4:8).

Perhaps John, who often referred to himself by the interesting phrase "the disciple Jesus loved" (John 13:23; 19:26; 20:2; 21:7, 20), said it best: "We love because he first loved us" (1 John 4:19).

BIBLICAL COMMANDS TO CHRISTIANS

Commands to Christians

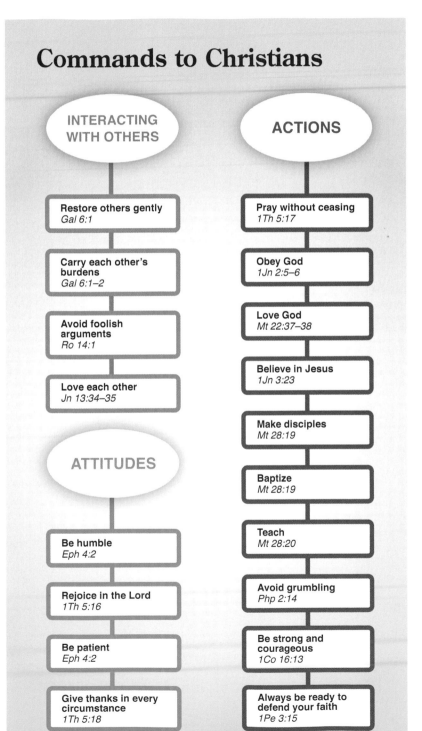

INTERACTING WITH OTHERS

Restore others gently
Gal 6:1

Carry each other's burdens
Gal 6:1–2

Avoid foolish arguments
Ro 14:1

Love each other
Jn 13:34–35

ATTITUDES

Be humble
Eph 4:2

Rejoice in the Lord
1Th 5:16

Be patient
Eph 4:2

Give thanks in every circumstance
1Th 5:18

ACTIONS

Pray without ceasing
1Th 5:17

Obey God
1Jn 2:5–6

Love God
Mt 22:37–38

Believe in Jesus
1Jn 3:23

Make disciples
Mt 28:19

Baptize
Mt 28:19

Teach
Mt 28:20

Avoid grumbling
Php 2:14

Be strong and courageous
1Co 16:13

Always be ready to defend your faith
1Pe 3:15

CROSS-REFERENCES

Deuteronomy 10:19

1 Corinthians 13:13

1 Thessalonians 3:12

CHAPTER 70

No topic has been explored by songwriters more than *love*. And while songs like "Something" by the Beatles, "Through the Years" by Kenny Rogers, and "I Will Always Love You" by Whitney Houston generated a lot of album sales, none of these pop culture songs have been able to fully provide a faithful description of true love.

What does the *Bible* say about love to our love-starved world?

Love originates in God. God's essential nature is love (1 John 4:8, 16). This means that everything he does stems from love and is entirely consistent with his love. And since God is infinite, his love is endless.

Love is essentially selfless. The attributes of love praised by the apostle Paul in 1 Corinthians 13 have an "other" focus. True love isn't proud and boastful—it is protective and patient and kind. It seeks the good of the other. In other words, real love is selfless.

Think about this: when God—the one who *is* love—decided to reveal himself to the world (John 1:18), he did so by sending Jesus, a selfless servant. If we watch Jesus closely, we get a front-row seat to how love is supposed to work. In the Gospels we see Jesus serving others constantly. In the end we see him giving himself as a sacrifice. Jesus not only said, "Greater love has no one than this: to lay down one's life for one's friends" (John 15:13), he modeled it.

Love begets love. The apostle John said, "We love because he first loved us" (1 John 4:19). When God's love breaks through to us, that is, when we understand that we are—right now—loved unconditionally, totally, perfectly, passionately, and eternally, we no longer have to move through the world frantically trying to *get* love. Instead, we are free to *give* love to others. We realize we're safe in God's endless love, and so we become conduits of it.

Love requires action. Compassionate feelings are fine; they're just not enough. Mushy words have their place, but true love transcends talk. First John 3:18 says, "Dear children, let us not love with words or speech but with actions and in truth." And notice that John 3:16 doesn't read, "For God so loved the world, he felt downright awful about the world's plight." No, God *acted*. His love prompted him to give his Son, Jesus.

Life Application

Ask God to help you better understand his miraculous, life-changing love (even though, as Paul said, it's beyond our knowing [Ephesians 3:19]). Then think of two concrete ways you could selflessly demonstrate God's love to two people he has placed in your life.

WHAT IS GENUINE LOVE?

Kind   *Does not delight in evil*   **Never fails**

Keeps no record of wrongs   **Is not self-seeking**

Always trusts   **Rejoices with the truth**

Greater than faith or hope

Always protects

ATTRIBUTES OF LOVE

1 Corinthians 13:4–13

Does not boast

Does not envy   *Always perseveres*

Does not dishonor others   **Is not easily angered**

Patient   *Is not proud*   **Always hopes**

CROSS-REFERENCES

Mark 12:28–31

Romans 8:31–39

1 Thessalonians 3:12

CHAPTER 71

One of the recurring teachings of the Bible is that our outer conduct is tied to our inner condition (Proverbs 4:23; Mark 7:21–23). A good heart means a good life. Bad roots yield bad fruit.

The apostle Paul talked about this reality in his letter to the Galatian Christians. He was urging them to remember that we are made right with God by faith alone. And so he was arguing that forgiven children of God shouldn't give in to *legalism* (i.e., anxiously trying to earn God's favor by keeping his law; Galatians 5:1–12), nor to *license* (i.e., living any way we please; 5:13–15). Rather, we are called to a life of faith under the glorious control of God's Spirit (5:16–26).

What can we expect in such a life? At least two things:

Conflict. Paul reminds us here that even though the Spirit of God Almighty indwells every believer, we still wrestle with our "flesh." (Our flesh is our fallen, irredeemable human nature. In salvation, God doesn't "upgrade" that old sinful nature; he gives us a new nature by making us new creatures in Christ; 2 Corinthians 5:17). This is why we struggle in our souls (Galatians 5:17). Every moment of every day we face this question: Will I allow myself to be led by the unholy desires of my flesh or by the holy promptings of the Spirit of God?

Fruit. Paul says that depending on the choice we make, we will see results that are "obvious" (Galatians 5:19). The deeds of the flesh (5:19–21) make for an ugly, regrettable life. But the life of a Spirit-led person will be marked by the beautiful fruit of the Spirit: "love, joy, peace, forbearance, kindness, goodness, faithfulness, gentleness and self-control" (5:22–23). One chapter earlier, Paul talks about this same idea in a different way—as the character of Christ being formed in our lives (4:19).

Life Application

What do you notice about your life? Are you joyful? Peaceful? Marked by forbearance (i.e., patience with trying people and tough situations)? If so, praise the Lord. Such spiritual fruit is his doing, not yours. Continue to invite the Spirit to animate your every action.

On the other hand, if your thoughts, words, and deeds are riddled with worry, impurity, hatred, envy, selfish ambition, and anger, ask God to forgive you—and to help you address those deeper issues of your heart.

CULTIVATING THE FRUIT OF THE SPIRIT

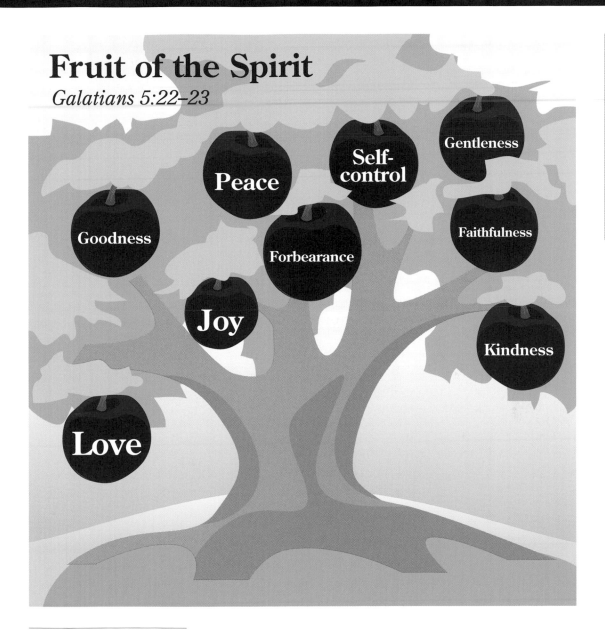

Fruit of the Spirit
Galatians 5:22–23

Gentleness

Peace

Self-control

Goodness

Forbearance

Faithfulness

Joy

Kindness

Love

CROSS-REFERENCES

Matthew 13:8

Ephesians 5:9

2 Peter 1:5–7

CHAPTER 72

Ephesians consists of three eye-popping chapters of our riches in Christ followed by three practical chapters of our responsibilities to Christ. Near the end of the letter, Paul mentions the somber reality of spiritual warfare. Speaking of "the devil's schemes" and "our struggle . . . against the spiritual forces of evil," he urges, "Put on the full armor of God" (6:11–12).

Scholars believe that Paul was under house arrest in Rome when he wrote these words—guarded constantly by an armed Roman soldier. Surely this experience inspired Paul's military imagery for how to "stand firm" (6:14) in the faith.

Have **"the belt of truth"** buckled around your waist, Paul urges (6:14). A soldier's leather belt provided a place to hang his sword and a means for cinching up his loose tunic (in order to be unhindered while fighting or marching). Paul's point seems to be that when we allow God's truth to both surround and shape our lives, we develop integrity—which brings security (see Proverbs 10:9).

Make sure **"the breastplate of righteousness"** is in place, Paul says (6:14). These ancient "flak jackets" were made of leather and covered in metal plates or chainmail. They provided protection for a warrior's vital organs—neck to waist and front to back. The implication is that by putting on (and living out) the righteousness that is given us in Christ (Romans 5:19), we are shielded from sin's evil consequences.

Noting the hobnailed sandals laced around the ankles and shins of his guard, Paul adds that a believer's feet should be **"fitted with the readiness that comes from the gospel of peace"** (6:15). It's by standing strong in the gospel that we find firm footing in a war-torn world. The gospel gives us (and those we share it with) peaceful, stable lives.

Paul speaks of **"the shield of faith"** (6:16). This large, either round or rectangular piece of wood was covered in animal skin and bound with iron. When wetted, it helped "extinguish all the flaming arrows" (6:16)

Life Application

Spend a few minutes prayerfully "putting on the full armor of God." For example, *Lord, guard my mind with your great salvation; help me to stand strong in the gospel today.* In a situation where you feel overwhelmed and like quitting, hold up the shield of faith by trusting in a promise like "I can do all this through him who gives me strength" (Philippians 4:13).

PROTECTING YOURSELF WITH GOD'S ARMOR

fired by the enemy. Paul is suggesting that by trusting in God's character and promises, we are shielded from assaults by the enemy.

"The helmet of salvation" (6:17) brings to mind Roman helmets made of iron or bronze and lined with cloth or sponge. These were sometimes decorated with distinctive plumes or markings. The idea is that by knowing and understanding our true identity and destiny, Christians can avoid becoming casualties.

Finally, Paul mentions an offensive weapon—and what a weapon it is: **"the sword of the Spirit, which is the word of God"** (6:17). By rightly handling Scripture, we are able—like Jesus in Matthew 4—to parry the enemy's blows and strike back at his demonic lies with eternal truth.

CROSS-REFERENCES

1 Thessalonians 5:8

2 Timothy 2:3–4

James 4:7

Armor of God
Ephesians 6:10–17

Sword of the Spirit

Helmet of salvation

Breastplate of righteousness

Belt of truth

Shield of faith

Feet fitted with readiness

CHAPTER 73

We're living in the "information age." Experts say that knowledge (i.e., the sum total of what the human race knows) doubles every year. So, for example, if we decided today that we'd like to print out and learn everything that's on the Internet (all four and a half billion pages of it), we'd first need to cut down sixteen million trees just to have enough copy paper for our project.

Knowledge, facts, intelligence—there's no shortage of all that. What the world lacks and needs more of is *wisdom*.

What is wisdom? To the ancient Hebrews, wisdom wasn't knowledge (as we typically think of the word). It was "skill in living rightly." It was knowledge *applied to life*. We could differentiate the two ideas in this way:

Knowledge	Wisdom
Acquired in the *lecture*	Cultivated in the *laboratory* of real life
Information	Insight
More conceptual	More practical/ relational/applicable
Focuses on *learning* what's *true*	Focuses on *doing* what's *right*
More of a *head* issue	More of a *heart* issue

Both knowledge and wisdom are necessary. Without knowledge we'd have nothing to apply. But without wisdom, a person could have a 200 IQ *and* advanced degrees from Harvard and MIT, and still be an absolute fool. Novelist Walker Percy put it this way: "You can get all A's and still flunk life."

Where does wisdom come from? "The *fear of the LORD* is the beginning of wisdom," says Proverbs 9:10 (emphasis added).

"Fear" in the Old Testament often refers to abject terror. However, when used in contexts like this one, it conveys the idea of "reverence." It is awe and wonder more than panic. (Though, to be sure, those who encounter God in Scripture almost always hug the ground for dear life.) In short, to fear the Lord is to be filled with deep reverence for him.

Life Application

Could you use some wisdom? Then begin to grow in wisdom by cultivating a healthy fear of the Lord. It only makes sense to revere God! Consider: he made you, loves you, sustains you, calls you, seeks you, saves you, blesses you, owns you, is with you, disciplines you, transforms you, gifts you, uses you, and will one day assess and reward you.

There is no better place to find what we need most than from the One who possesses "all the treasures of wisdom and knowledge" (Colossians 2:3).

WHAT IS WISDOM?

7 Pillars of Wisdom

Proverbs 8:12–14; 9:1

LIVING AS A CHRISTIAN

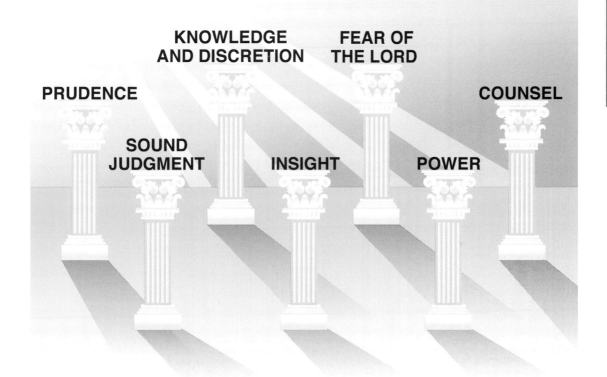

KNOWLEDGE
AND DISCRETION

FEAR OF
THE LORD

PRUDENCE

COUNSEL

SOUND
JUDGMENT

INSIGHT

POWER

CROSS-REFERENCES

Proverbs 4:7

Daniel 2:20

James 3:13–18

CHAPTER 74

Everybody has problems. And most problems tend to fall into one of the following areas: getting along with others, working, handling money, living in a sex-obsessed world, and trying to be a person of character (and/or suffering negative consequences when one fails to live with integrity).

Given this reality, it's not surprising that the Old Testament book of Proverbs is one of the Bible's most popular books. It is timeless and speaks powerfully and practically to common, everyday situations.

The Proverbs are a collection of wise sayings (ascribed primarily to King Solomon; see 1:1). They are moral and ethical observations about the way the world generally works. They are not so much guarantees or iron-clad promises (we can always find exceptions to a proverb). But they are trustworthy maxims and tested truisms. They're beloved because they are so memorable, short, and compelling.

The overriding purpose of the collection is stated up front (1:2–4): to grant insight and to encourage people to embrace a disciplined life by showing the stark difference between the way the wise and the foolish live. Since the word translated "proverb" probably comes from a Hebrew word that means "to be like," many of the proverbs consist of simple comparisons. Here's a sampling from each of the book's most popular categories:

- **Character.** "Whoever walks in integrity walks securely, but whoever takes crooked paths will be found out" (10:9).
- **Money and business.** "All hard work brings a profit, but mere talk leads only to poverty" (14:23).
- **Spiritual health.** "The LORD is far from the wicked, but he hears the prayer of the righteous" (15:29).
- **Relationships.** "Wounds from a friend can be trusted, but an enemy multiplies kisses" (27:6).
- **Choosing wise words.** "The words of the reckless pierce like swords, but the tongue of the wise brings healing" (12:18).
- **Temptation and sex.** "Can a man walk on hot coals without his feet being scorched? So is he who sleeps with another man's wife; no one who touches her will go unpunished" (6:28–29).

Life Application

Take a month to read the book of Proverbs. At thirty-one chapters, that's just one chapter a day.

DOWN-TO-EARTH WISDOM FROM PROVERBS

Topics in Proverbs

Main themes found in Proverbs

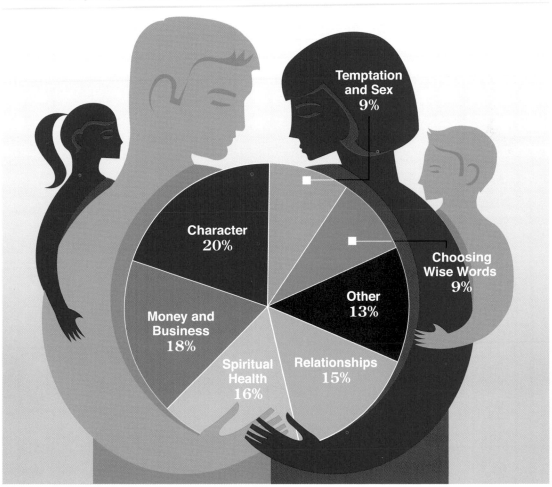

Temptation and Sex 9%

Character 20%

Choosing Wise Words 9%

Other 13%

Money and Business 18%

Spiritual Health 16%

Relationships 15%

CROSS-REFERENCES

Ecclesiastes

James

CHAPTER 75

The book of Proverbs is a treasury of down-to-earth wisdom compiled by the wisest man—other than Jesus—ever to live (1 Kings 3:10–12). Proverbs highlights the practical differences between godliness and wickedness, between the way wise people and foolish people live.

What Foolishness Is

Using three different Hebrew words, the book of Proverbs mentions *fools* more than sixty times. In the biblical view, *foolishness* has more of an ethical than an intellectual meaning. It's about character, not IQ. Put simply, Proverbs considers any person who does not fear God (i.e., live reverently and humbly before him) a fool. What's more, apart from earnestly seeking and acquiring *wisdom* (the moral insight or "skill in living" provided by God and his Word; see Proverbs 4:5–7), a person's life is sure to be marked by pride and regrettable, foolish behavior.

How to Spot a Fool

Proverbs mentions many of the most common behaviors of fools: They are, for example, disinterested in the things of God (1:7). They are complacent (1:32). They are quick to quarrel (20:3) and rage at others (29:11). They resist making amends (14:9).

However, Proverbs emphasizes two enormous character flaws that shout to the world, "This person is a fool!"

1. *Reckless speech habits*. Proverbs shows how fools make no attempt to guard their tongues—they lie (10:18), mock (23:9), are argumentative (18:6), talk without thinking (29:20) or listening (18:2), lash out with pride (14:3), and just generally spout stupidity (14:7; 15:2).

2. *Unwillingness to take correction*. Time and again, Proverbs says that foolish people bristle when others attempt to show them a wiser way to live. They resent and reject any kind of constructive criticism or advice (1:7; 12:1, 15; 13:18; 15:5, 32; 17:10; 23:9; 27:22).

Why Foolishness Needs to Be Forsaken

What does the future look like for foolish people? According to Proverbs, it's pretty grim. The fool who refuses to change his or her ways is headed for shame (3:35), ruin (10:8, 10, 14), and eventually death (10:21; 14:12; 16:25).

FOOLISH TALK

How to Spot a Fool
Proverbs

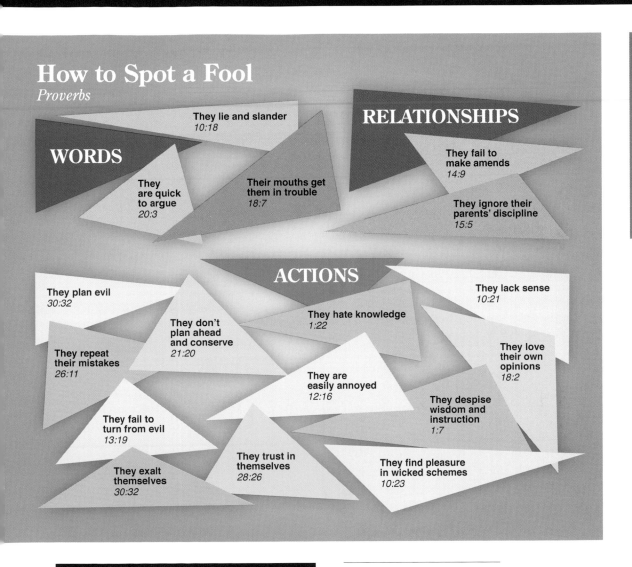

WORDS

They lie and slander
10:18

They
are quick
to argue
20:3

Their mouths get
them in trouble
18:7

RELATIONSHIPS

They fail to
make amends
14:9

They ignore their
parents' discipline
15:5

ACTIONS

They plan evil
30:32

They don't
plan ahead
and conserve
21:20

They hate knowledge
1:22

They lack sense
10:21

They repeat
their mistakes
26:11

They love
their own
opinions
18:2

They are
easily annoyed
12:16

They despise
wisdom and
instruction
1:7

They fail to
turn from evil
13:19

They exalt
themselves
30:32

They trust in
themselves
28:26

They find pleasure
in wicked schemes
10:23

Walk with the wise and become wise, for a companion of fools suffers harm.

Proverbs 13:20

CROSS-REFERENCES

Job 5:2

Psalm 14:1

Ecclesiastes 5:4

CHAPTER 76

In most settings leaders are picked because they are intelligent, well-spoken, well-connected, good-looking, rich, or influential.

In two separate New Testament letters, the apostle Paul gives a different (and daunting) set of qualifications for those who would lead in the church. One list is found in Titus 1:5–9 (pictured at right). First Timothy 3:1–7 provides a similar list:

- "Above reproach" (v. 2) means without the kind of glaring character flaws that raise eyebrows; it's synonymous with "blameless" in the Titus list.
- "Faithful to his wife" (v. 2) is translated "a one-woman man" by some scholars and suggests sexual/moral purity.
- "Temperate" (v. 2) means sober-minded, well-balanced, or levelheaded—not given to extremes.
- "Self-controlled" (v. 2) suggests leaders who are thoughtful or prudent—the opposite of impulsive.
- "Respectable" (v. 2) calls for leaders whom others are "able to respect" because they fulfill their duties out of an upright life.
- "Hospitable" (v. 2) means generous and gracious, willing to share their lives and resources.
- "Able to teach" (v. 2) means competence in understanding and explaining the Bible.

- "Not given to drunkenness" (v. 3) rules out chemical addictions.
- "Not violent but gentle" (v. 3) negates bullies and those given to fits of rage.
- "Not quarrelsome" (v. 3) eliminates from leadership consideration those who like to stir up conflict.
- "Not a lover of money" (v. 3) isn't a prohibition of people with means, only those who are obsessed with their wealth.
- "Must manage his own family well" (v. 4) is based on the question of verse 5, "If anyone does not know how to manage his own family, how can he take care of God's church?"
- "Must not be a recent convert" (v. 6) is a stipulation intended to guard against immaturity and pride.
- "Must also have a good reputation with outsiders" (v. 7) is the requirement that a leader be respected in the community as one with integrity.

Most of these characteristics are extolled elsewhere in the Bible for all people who follow Jesus. While mature Christians are to exhibit these traits—and to work at growing in them—the Bible says that pastors, elders, and bishops should especially reflect them.

WHO SHOULD LEAD THE CHURCH?

Qualifications of a Church Leader
Titus 1:5–9

An elder must be ...

Blameless

Faithful in marriage

Raising children who believe

Raising children who are not wild and disobedient

Hospitable

One who loves what is good

Self-controlled

Upright

Holy

Disciplined

A firm believer in the gospel

Encouraging to others

Willing to refute those who oppose the gospel

An elder must not be ...

Overbearing

Quick-tempered

Given to drunkenness

Violent

Dishonest

Life Application

Pray for your own church leaders. Their load (shepherding the eternal souls of a group of people who are full of hurts and hopes) is heavy. Pray for grace, peace, endurance, and joy. Second, pray for your own heart. Perhaps God will never call you to lead a church body. But at least pray for the character to do so if called.

CROSS-REFERENCES
Psalm 15

Acts 20:17–38

2 Timothy 2:20–26